Why Hasn't He Proposed?

Why Hasn't He Proposed?

Go from the First Date to Setting the Date

MATT TITUS & TAMSEN FADAL

New York   Chicago   San Francisco   Lisbon   London   Madrid   Mexico City
Milan   New Delhi   San Juan   Seoul   Singapore   Sydney   Toronto

Library of Congress Cataloging-in-Publication Data

Titus, Matt.
    Why hasn't he proposed? : go from the first date to setting the date / Matt Titus
and Tamsen Fadal.
       p.   cm.
    Includes bibliographical references and index.
    ISBN-13: 978-0-07-161496-2 (alk. paper)
    ISBN-10: 0-07-161496-6
    1. Man-woman relationships.   2. Men—Psychology.   3. Women—
Psychology.   4. Dating (Social customs).   5. Betrothal.   I. Fadal,
Tamsen.   II. Title.

HQ801.T4994   2009
646.7'7082—dc22   2008042539

1 2 3 4 5 6 7 8 9 10 11 12 13 14 15 16 17 18 19 20 21 22   FGR/FGR   0 9 8

ISBN   978-0-07-161496-2
MHID   0-07-161496-6

McGraw-Hill books are available at special quantity discounts to use as premiums and
sales promotions or for use in corporate training programs. To contact a representative,
please visit the Contact Us pages at www.mhprofessional.com.

This book is printed on acid-free paper.

To my late mother, Libby, who taught me
how to love and how to be loved.

And, to my father, Jim, and my brother, Cristan, who
are my rocks in life and made me who I am today.

And to my loving husband, Matt, who inspires me with his
love every day as my soul mate, partner, and best friend.

To my late mother, Faith, who I wish could
have seen me become a man.

And to my father, Paul, who is not only a
supportive dad but also my friend.

And to my loving wife, Tamsen, whose energy and love
are never ending. You have changed my life forever.

CONTENTS

ACKNOWLEDGMENTS

We believe that relationships are what matter in life. Our relationships with so many loving and supportive people helped make *Why Hasn't He Proposed?* and, before that, *Why Hasn't He Called?* possible for the millions of people who deserve true love.

First and foremost, the inspiration, love, and support of our families made this book a reality. They listened patiently to our ideas, thoughts, and dreams at every family outing, over dinners, through the holidays, and during all phone conversations! We don't know how you have put up with us all this time, but we want to say thank you: Dad and Carol Fadal, Cristan and Jen Fadal, and Dad Titus, you continue to believe in us and inspire us with your unconditional love.

To our closest friends, Andrew Ackerman, Diane Hockstein, Rob Pearson, and Mike and Dianna Feldman, thank you for always being there to motivate us and help us reach our dreams.

Why Hasn't He Proposed? would not have come to be without the words of Bonnie Bauman, who believes in our message and knew exactly how to bring our voice to life, not only as a writer and editor but also as a constant supporter, cheerleader, and friend.

A very, very special thanks to Carol Mann, our agent and friend, who not only fields a million phone calls a week every time we have a thought or feeling but also believes in us and our vision.

Sincere thanks are likewise due to Karen Kelly, who knew we were supposed to write this book even before we knew and made sure it happened in the real proposal, and to Johanna Bowman, who knew we had a second book in us!

Beth Feldman, who goes above and "beyond," thank you for standing by us as this book was being written and helping us deliver its message.

The same to Sarah Pelz, who jumped right in at the last minute to bring *Why Hasn't He Proposed?* to all those who are waiting for that big rock! Plus, we couldn't have done it without all the special folks at McGraw-Hill; thank you for believing in us once again.

And a big kiss to our Chihuahuas, Matsen and Parker, who sacrificed trips to Central Park as they waited patiently for this book to be completed!

Finally, we are most grateful to our WhyHasntHe.com readers and our loyal "Matched in Manhattan" fans who continue to share their stories with us so that we can help others who wonder how men really think!

Remember, if you need us, we are only an e-mail away at Ask@WhyHasntHe.com.

INTRODUCTION

Dear Matt and Tamsen,

I've been in a serious relationship with a man for two years. I'm very much in love with him, and he says he feels the same way about me. We have a lot in common, we have a great time together, and the sex is amazing. The best part of our relationship is that the spark between us has never dimmed—I still get butterflies when he walks into the room. I'm completely committed to our relationship, and he seems every bit as into it as I am.

Here's the problem: he hasn't proposed! On my end, I have no doubt that he's the guy I want to spend the rest of my life with, but the closest he's gotten to bringing up the "M" word with me is the time he asked me to go with him to his best friend's wedding. I'm hesitant to be the one to bring up marriage, because I'm afraid it will scare him away. Plus, I want him to *want* to marry me! I want the surprise dropping down on one knee and the offering up of the little velvet box with the shiny diamond ring inside. I want to hear the nervous uncertainty in his voice when he asks me to be his wife and feel the relief in his embrace when I say: "Yes!"

What I don't want is to have to make a federal case out of the whole thing! So, between my fear and pride and his evasiveness, the topic has never come up. That doesn't mean it isn't starting to come between us. Lately, it's been like the giant pink elephant in the room; I know he knows I'm thinking about it, and he knows I know he's avoiding the subject.

To make matters worse, it seems as if everyone around me is getting engaged. If one more person asks me when it's going to be "my turn" at one more wedding that isn't mine, or if I have to buy one more expensive gift from Pottery Barn for some other couple's future together, I'm going to lose it!

Matt and Tamsen, why hasn't he proposed?! And what can I do to get the ball rolling and get a ring on my finger?!

Thank you in advance for your help!

Molly

 "Why hasn't he proposed?" It's not just a clever book title Tamsen and I came up with; it's a genuine question we've heard countless times in the past couple of years as our business has evolved from a match-

making gig into a full-fledged relationship coaching operation. What I've learned from counseling clients on this topic is that while there isn't one static answer we can give to Molly and to every other woman who finds herself in this predicament, there is a list of universal reasons behind the hesitation men are feeling these days about popping the question. In nearly every situation we've come across, one or more of these reasons can be circled.

In this book, we offer a full explanation of each of these reasons along with actionable steps a woman can take to get her guy over whatever preproposal hump or humps he's struggling with. Each chapter gives women guidance on what they should or *shouldn't* be doing to get their guy past his hang-ups and on to the honeymoon. In our business, Tamsen and I pride ourselves on being straightforward and honest with our clients—often painfully so. We bring that same tough love to the pages of this book. In addition to giving women the reasons their guy hasn't proposed, we'll help them spot the red flags that signal that the guy they want to exchange vows with isn't worth exchanging the time of day with. Here's a little taste of what's between the covers:

- A timetable that will tell you exactly when it's time for him to pop the question.
- If and when you should bring up the "M" word, and advice on the best way to broach the topic.
- The dangers of cohabitation before marriage, as well as the right and wrong way to shack up.

- The top reasons why he's terrified of marriage. For instance, one of his biggest fears is having sex with only one woman for the rest of his life. For that reason, we've devoted an entire chapter to how you're going to show him why that's a good thing!

- What you can do to calm all of his fears of marriage without ever letting him know you were the one who put them to rest.

- Signals that he's not the guy you're meant to marry.

- All of the important issues that must be addressed once he does go down on one knee, so that you can start your life as husband and wife on solid footing.

Just what gives us the audacity to call ourselves experts on this particular topic? I'll let my gorgeous new bride tackle that question.

 The reason Matt and I believe we can shed light on the issue we've dubbed "male altarphobia" is that for the past several years we've devoted ourselves to helping women and men establish and maintain healthy, happy, and fulfilling relationships. We've coached couples through good times, bad times, and everything in between. We've seen it all! And we've decided to share everything we've uncovered about male altarphobia in the pages of this book.

Another thing that makes our perspective on the topic worth taking to heart is that we're a *couple* working to keep couples together. Because of this dynamic, we've had the opportunity to educate one another in a unique way. Matt gives me the male perspective, and I give him the female take on things. As a result, each of us tends to walk away from the many different dating and relationship scenarios we come across with a deeper understanding of the situation. I believe this depth of understanding gives the advice and guidance in this book a level of accuracy and truth that an author writing alone on the topic could not provide.

Speaking of writing, much has changed since we wrote and published our last book, *Why Hasn't He Called?* If you missed that one, allow me to give you some brief background info on Matt and me. I'll also fill you in on how the matchmaking business that prompted us to write that first book together has evolved into a comprehensive dating/relationship coaching operation.

For his part, Matt's been in the relationship biz for five years now. He wasn't always the stand-up guy he is now. In another life, he was the ultimate player. He was married to a lovely woman but was playing the field. After a near-fatal motorcycle accident drove him to own up to his cheating ways, he found himself divorced, broke, and full of self-loathing. Always one to turn a negative into a positive, he decided to use his bad fortune as an opportunity to learn from his mistakes and become a better person. Following a period of soul-searching, he vowed never to cheat on another woman as long as he lived.

He also decided that he wanted to use his knowledge of the inner workings of the male brain to help women instead of hurt them. This desire is what led him to open a matchmaking business, in which he began helping women understand the male mind in order to improve their chances of meeting Mr. Right. He opened his business in Manhattan, the ultimate dating scene. By then he had taken a dose of his own matchmaking advice and fallen in love with the woman of his dreams—me!

When Matt and I first met back in Philly, I was a successful journalist with an Emmy under my belt. Nevertheless, I was earning no props when it came to dating and relationships. I had a bad case of the female version of altarphobia and was determined to steer clear of any relationship that had a future. Then I met Matt. Although I did my best to scare him off, he was persistent. Plus, OK, I'll admit it: I was smitten from the instant I laid eyes on the guy. The next thing I knew, he was down on one knee, and I was cosigning a lease for an apartment with a spectacular view of the New York City skyline!

From the get-go, I was fascinated by Matt's business. I loved it when he asked me for advice on a match or asked my opinion on a new client. The first time my input succeeded in making a match, I was hooked. I had found a new calling. Before I knew it, I was a full-fledged partner in the business, and Matt and I were filming and starring in a Lifetime reality series about our matchmaking business and personal lives as a married couple, aptly named "Matched in Manhattan," not to mention writing a book together!

Neither of us could have predicted the phenomenal impact that first book was to have on our business and our lives. The moment it hit the bookstores, we began receiving thousands of e-mails and letters from people asking for dating and relationship advice. In response, we built our very own website at WhyHasntHe.com to answer the flood of questions coming our way. We also began making regular television and radio appearances, hosting our own Internet show on paltalk.com, and holding regular dating/relationship boot camps for men and women.

By far the best change in our lives took place at the altar during our beautiful wedding ceremony. On October 13, 2007, at Tavern on the Green in Central Park, Matt and I said "I do," and Matt officially became Mr. Tamsen Fadal! Make no mistake: our marriage has been no fairy-tale ending. On the contrary, it's been a *real-life beginning.* Our life as wife and husband has been full of ups and downs and all the stuff in between. With this book, we hope to give you the advice you need to make sure you aren't looking for a proposal from Mr. Wrong and instead are ready for a real-life beginning with your Mr. Right.

RELATIONSHIP LIMBO

Nicole and Mike have been together for three years. Nicole, 30, and Mike, 29, met in their hometown of Austin, Texas. It was one of those relationships that just naturally fall into place. They met at a party, exchanged phone numbers, went out on a first date, and within a month were officially exclusive. After they had been dating for about a year, Mike got a job offer from a top ad agency in New York City. Still very much in the throes of new love, he wasn't about to leave Nicole behind, so he asked her to make the move with him. Nicole, a photographer, had always dreamed of living in New York City, so a chance to relocate to the Big Apple with a guy with whom she was madly in love wasn't exactly a hard sell. Cohabitation came with the relocation package. New York City's outrageously high cost of living meant that renting separate apartments wasn't an option.

At the time, neither Nicole nor Mike brought up the topic of marriage. For Mike's part, it didn't occur to him to bring it up. Many of the couple's friends and family members, on the other hand, assumed that by asking Nicole to move with him to New York, Mike was laying the groundwork for an eventual proposal. However, at 26, Mike was focused on establishing his career, and even though he was in love with Nicole, getting married was the furthest thing from his mind. Sure, being with Nicole made him happy, at times downright giddy, but he was a guy; it wasn't as if he sat around mulling where their relationship was ultimately headed or what Nicole was thinking.

As for Nicole, deep down she *did* wonder about what Mike was contemplating, where the relationship was going, and whether the move together would ultimately lead to marriage. (After all, she was a girl.) At that point in the relationship, though, they were just passing thoughts. These musings had yet to take root in her brain and mature into hopes and fears. In those early days of the relationship, her brain was still awash with all the chemicals that are released by new love. She was too busy being elated about having found her soul mate and too excited about living in New York City to worry about whether the move would lead to marriage.

It was a good thing she wasn't hung up on marriage, because if she had been, she would have found herself in a major dilemma. As with many other Southern women, Nicole was full of contradictions regarding men and relationships. She wasn't so old-fashioned that she would abstain from premarital sex or refuse to move in with a boyfriend, but when it came to subjects such as marriage, she felt it was the man's place to bring up the topic, not the woman's.

Two years later, with many New York City adventures behind them, Mike still hadn't brought up the subject of marriage, and Nicole had remained true to her Southern upbringing and never broached the topic. The problem was that by now the fogginess of new love had lifted, and with a clear head, not to mention a ticking biological clock, Nicole was thinking seriously about her future with Mike—more like obsessing about it. After two years of cohabitation, she was still crazy in love with Mike, and there wasn't a doubt in her mind that he was the man she wanted to marry. Mike seemed equally happy. Why shouldn't he be? The chemistry was still there, the sex was as hot as ever, and the good times and laughs were still coming. So, why hadn't Mike proposed? What was his *problem*? With each passing month, Nicole began to feel more and more that she was in a state of limbo and that there were only two ways out: a proposal from Mike or a breakup.

• • • • • • • • • • • • • LIMBO LAND • • • • • • • • • • • • •

 Nicole is not alone in relationship limbo; hundreds of thousands of other equally fabulous women are right there with her—all wanting to take their relationships forward but stuck by their boyfriends' inaction. Typically, a woman winds up in this state of limbo two to three years into an otherwise healthy relationship. Here are a few signposts that point to the conclusion that your

relationship has veered off course and is now parked in limbo land:

- You've created a mental spreadsheet of all the married couples you know, with the exact amount of time it took each couple to get from their meeting day to their wedding day.
- Occasions that used to be fun have now become uncomfortable, such as Valentine's Day, your anniversary, and any wedding that the two of you are invited to attend.
- Many things that he says or does have become clouded over by your feelings of impatience and disappointment in his not having proposed. For instance, if he gets a raise, you think, "Great, now you can afford to buy me a ring, buddy!" Or if he buys you flowers, you think, "Enough with the flowers already; think 'carats!' "
- Because of your frustration, one-on-one time with him has become strained and uncomfortable. As a consequence, you both manage to either avoid being alone together or make sure there are enough diversions to drown out the awkwardness. For instance, the television is always on during dinner at home, friends always accompany you when you eat out, and you can't remember the last time you both just sat outside and shot the breeze during sunset.

If these signs sound all too familiar, have no fear! Tamsen and I are here to guide you out of relationship limbo. But before I go any further, I want you to fully understand that you're not alone. I have the numbers to prove it! Just check out these stats: From 1995 to 2005, the marriage rate in the United States dropped by nearly 20 percent, according to a Rutgers University study. Moreover, in 2007, it was reported that for the first time ever, more American women (51 percent) were unmarried than were married.

Don't misunderstand: I don't think there's anything wrong with a woman's choosing not to marry or to live with a long-term boyfriend in lieu of getting hitched. The distressing element is that many women who are unmarried today are not *choosing* to be spouseless. Quite the contrary: a large number of them are simply waiting for long-term boyfriends to pop the question. The proof is in my in-box. Every day I receive e-mails from women all over the country who are frustrated by their boyfriends' disinterest in marriage. These women say they are with the men with whom they want to spend the rest of their lives, but the guys just don't seem interested in taking them as lawfully wedded wives.

 WHY I ASKED HER . . .

I knew Athena was the one because she was me with all the right parts. She loves sports, she is easygoing when we are together, and she is independent. Plus, we have the same values: we put life before money and put happiness before success.

—*Rob, married to Athena for four years*

••••••••• STATE OF DISUNION ••••••••

 Before we get into listing the reasons he's not pro-
posing, I'd like to talk a little about the current state
of marriage. Believe it or not, this ancient institution
has seen more changes in the past thirty years than
it has in the past five thousand! One of the chief changes is
that both men and women are waiting longer to get married.
Here are some more numbers for you: the marriage rate has
dropped by about 30 percent in the past twenty-five years, and
on average, Americans are waiting about five years longer to
marry than they did back in 1970. In New York, it's as rare to
find someone in his or her twenties who's married as it is to
find a cab on a rainy day during rush hour.

One reason people are saying, "I don't right now" instead
of "I do" is that they're choosing to head higher up the corporate ladder before they go down the aisle. Both men and
women are putting marriage on the back burner to focus more
on their careers. Unfortunately, by the time they get around
to looking for Mr. or Ms. Right, their dating pool is more like
a puddle. Putting marriage off is not necessarily a bad thing
either. In fact, waiting to marry might actually improve your
chances of having a successful union. Here's why:

▨ The older you are when you marry, the more wisdom you
have acquired. The wiser you are, the better your pros-
pects of weathering the many storms that come with
marriage.

▢ With age comes more self-assurance and a greater sense of independence.

▢ Couples who wait longer to marry are typically more financially stable.

▢ The criteria that folks who are older and wiser use to choose their marriage partners are concerned less with attraction and more with shared values, according to divorce360.com.

Another reason people aren't rushing to the altar today is that our society has come to accept cohabitation. Long-term couples who decide to live together without a legally recognized union are no longer looked down upon and accused of "living in sin"—except perhaps by grandparents and grand-aunts and -uncles. As a result, the number of couples shacking up has skyrocketed. Since 1970, the number of Americans living together has jumped from about five hundred thousand opposite-sex couples to more than five million, according to another Rutgers study.

One thing that's spurring this trend is the publicity given to many Hollywood couples who are going to the maternity ward without first stopping at the chapel. Think Angelina Jolie and Brad Pitt, Nicole Richie and Joel Madden, as well as Halle Berry and Naomi Watts and their respective baby daddies. For better or for worse, the goings-on in Hollywood have a tremendous impact on the trends that are embraced by our society. Here let me repeat my earlier disclaimer: there is nothing whatsoever wrong with choosing to cohabit as opposed to getting married. Then again, if your heart is set on eventually marrying your cohabitant, shacking up can thwart your chances of ever getting that marriage certificate. More on this in Chapter 2.

The last big impact on marriage that I'd like to touch on has to do with a bit of confusion left behind by the feminist movement. Don't get me wrong, ladies: I have no problem with feminism in any way, shape, or form. In fact, I embrace it—every day, as a matter of fact; no one exudes more girl power than Tamsen! My premise is that, like it or not, the changes brought about by the feminist movement have left many guys perplexed about their roles in relationships. Case in point: Back in the olden days, the trajectory to the altar was clear. The man did the courting while the woman sat back and allowed herself to be courted. By and large, the man pretty much called all the shots in the relationship. Note the words "love, honor, and *obey*." That was then, and this is now. These days, men and women tend to be equals in their relationships and make every important decision together.

By default, men no longer have the mind-set of sitting alone in the driver's seat. There's little wonder that not many of them are waking up one day and thinking, "It's time for me to go to the jewelry store, pay thousands of dollars for a ring for my girlfriend, and ask her to marry me. Oh, and I'm going to take this gigantic step without seeking any input from her whatsoever, even though she has always participated in every major decision involving our relationship."

I firmly believe that in many instances men are not proposing because they are simply unsure of how they're supposed
to navigate this confusing landscape—a landscape where society in some respects wants it both ways: equality between the
sexes, except when it comes time to pay for dinner, open a
door, or make a life-changing decision about when it's time to
get married. Pretty confusing state of affairs for us guys, don't
you think? Aw, don't worry; this is just one of the many murky
areas we're going to clear up for you in the coming chapters.

• • • • • • • NOT JUST A PIECE OF PAPER • • • • • • •

Throughout my dating career, I was one of those
girls who scoffed at marriage. Whenever the topic
of marriage came up with family or friends, I'd
breezily refer to it as "just a piece of paper." When
Matt and I started to get serious, I continued to express ambivalence toward matrimony. One time when he was in the room
while I was chatting with a friend on the telephone, I even
allowed him to overhear my "it's just a piece of paper" speech.
Big talk. Matt, being Matt, saw right through me!

You see, the truth is—once I met Matt, anyway—all of my
protestations about marriage were more for my benefit than
anyone else's. I was working hard to convince myself that I
couldn't care less if Matt stuck around or took the next train
to Anywhere Else. In my heart, however, more than anything,

I wanted to marry him. The reason I was putting up such a tough front was that my mother passed away when I was 20, and because of that devastating loss, I was dealing with my own fears of abandonment. Thankfully, Matt scaled the protective wall I had built around my heart and asked me to marry him anyway.

Now that I've joined the ranks of the happily married, I get that marriage is *not* just a piece of paper. It's a powerful commitment in which you get to weave your life with the life of the person you love. I still can't believe how lucky I am to get to share my ups, downs, and everything in between with Matt. When it comes to marriage, I've gone from a critic to a convert.

Speaking of critics, when Matt and I began working on this book, we both ran across our share of them. "A woman shouldn't sit around and worry about whether a man is going to propose to her," they said. Accompanying them were the predictable cries, "Why write a book about marriage? It's nothing more than a piece of paper!" Boy, did that sound familiar. While I understand where these naysayers are coming from, I don't think they understand where Matt and I are coming from, or the reason we decided to write this book. We don't believe that wanting to marry the man with whom you are in love and to make a life together is in any way an antifeminist sentiment. We don't believe that it means you aren't a strong and independent woman. We think it's an honest, natural desire. After all, as females, we are biologically wired to seek a secure home with our mates in order to protect the future of the species. It's undeniable to us that marriage is so much more than a piece of paper! It's an institution that comes with countless perks.

Still, I didn't want you to just take my word for how great marriage is and why you should feel perfectly OK about wanting to marry the man you love. To support my position, I decided to put my investigative reporter skills to work and once and for all answer the question: "What's so great about marriage?" When I began my research, I was astounded at the body of scientific evidence that had been established on the pros of marriage. It turns out that marriage is good for our health, our bank accounts, and our sanity! Here's a brief summary of what I found:

☐ **Got marriage?** A mountain of research shows that married people live longer, healthier lives. People who are happily married have better immune systems. If you're counting, being married adds four years to a woman's life and ten years to a man's life! Married folks also suffer less from psychological disorders such as depression and anxiety and are less likely to abuse alcohol and drugs. Scientists believe that this effect is directly related to the fact that marriage adds a fuller sense of meaning to people's lives.

☐ **Cha-ching!** Being married means a bigger bank account. It's been proven that married men earn from 10 to 50 percent more money than their unmarried counterparts. Although the exact reasons for this discrepancy are not entirely clear, researchers believe a major contributor might be that employers are biased toward married men, considering them to be more committed, stable, and productive. Women don't share in this particular perk because as they begin having children, on average, their earning power tends to decline. However, they do have a stake in the overall economic benefits of being married. Studies also show that married folks manage their money better and build bigger nest eggs together.

⌐ **Sex, sex, and more sex!** Married people have hotter and more frequent sex. Yep, it's true. Forget that myth about singles having all the chandelier-swinging sex. A principal cause is that if you're married, you're more likely to have sex in the first place. Nearly 25 percent of single guys and 30 percent of single women aren't even having sex. Married folks are also having more satisfying sex, according to research. One explanation is that married couples have spent time perfecting skills that please their partners.

⌐ **Will you be my next of kin?** If you're married, the law is on your side. In total, married couples have fourteen hundred legal rights in the United States, including being designated the "next of kin" for hospital visits, the ability to have joint insurance policies, numerous tax benefits, and the right to half of one another's assets.

⌐ **Oh, happy day!** Last, but certainly not least, studies show that married people report being happier than cohabiters, divorced people, or folks who have never been married. There are several reasons for this, but one that I found particularly interesting is that married couples tend to split all of life's tasks according to who is better suited to perform the particular job. For example, if a wife is better than her husband at managing money, she will take care of the bills, leaving the husband, who hates to deal with money, free of that particular chore. Similarly, if the wife hates to cook, and her husband loves to cook, he gets to do something he enjoys, and she gets out of doing something she spurns. It's so simple, but it's so true. It's not hard to infer some of the other reasons for the spike in happiness. Remember: people who are married are healthier and richer and are having a better time between the sheets.

WHY I ASKED HER . . .

Her laugh made me happy, and her attractiveness was always exciting, and her enthusiasm for life was so contagious that I had to ask her to marry me. How could I not?
—*Jim, married to Carol for thirteen years*

WHEN SHOULD YOU EXPECT A PROPOSAL?

We've talked about the state of marriage today, so you now have an accurate measure of the playing field. We've chatted about the pros of marriage to give you a better understanding of what you're playing for. Now it's time to chat about the clock you're up against. Exactly when should you expect a proposal from the guy with whom you've been in a long-term relationship?

Unfortunately, the timetable for when a guy should propose in a long-term relationship is a bit on the subjective side. Undeterred, we've tapped our experience with thousands of couples to establish guidance on when it's most appropriate for him to pop the question. Here goes: You should not expect a proposal until you've been together for at least a year and a half. If it's been two and a half years, and he hasn't mentioned marriage, it's time to get down to business. However, if he's in his twenties, he gets more flexibility. According to the U.S. Census Bureau, the median age for a first marriage for men is 27.1, and for women it's 25.3; add about three years for folks living in major cities, such as New York, Chicago, or Los Angeles. Once he hits 30, however, the game is on. Certain extenuating circumstances do exist even when he's in his thirties. For instance, he gets leeway if he's pursuing a secondary degree or is in the military. Note: prison or any other legal trouble is not an extenuating circumstance; it's a deal breaker!

THE SIX TOP REASONS
HE'S NOT PROPOSING

Our experiences with thousands of couples have allowed us to uncover the overriding reasons men are dragging their feet about walking down the aisle. Listed here are the top half dozen reasons we've found for proposal apathy. Keep in mind that more than one might apply to your guy.

1. Cohabitation has made him complacent.
2. He's afraid of losing his unmarried edge and fears that a marriage certificate will be a ticket to a life of boredom and ordinariness.
3. He hates the thought of becoming the clown in his own wedding circus.
4. The prospect of sleeping with only one woman for the rest of his life terrifies him.
5. He's afraid of losing his independence.
6. He's afraid the marriage will be a miserable failure that will end up in divorce court and she'll walk away with half his stuff.

Now . . . let the games begin. You asked the question, and in the following pages, you're going to get your answers. The remaining chapters will give you more in-depth information on each of the reasons just listed, along with advice on what you can do to help him overcome his marital hang-ups. As you proceed, take note of the various red flags we describe; if these are waving in your relationship, they may be a signal that he is not the guy you are meant to marry.

THE PITFALLS OF PLAYING HOUSE

With his shaggy dark hair and big, brown doe eyes, Joe, a 36-year-old Seattle native, looks more like an indie rocker than a chef. Today we meet up with Joe on a typical Monday morning. It's after 10:00 A.M., and he's just waking up. Joe's no slacker; he worked the late shift last night and didn't get in until well after midnight. After giving the cat some attention, Joe shuffles over to the coffeepot, where he finds a note from Rachael, his live-in girlfriend of about a year and a half.

"Morning, JoJo!" the note begins. "Happy rent day! Please put your check in the envelope on the fridge and mail it. From your half, deduct the $250 that I owe you for the vet bill! The guy is coming at noon to fix the TV. And reminder: Saturday is Grammie's 80th b-day party—start thinking of a gift idea. I'm going to run to the grocery after work today. Call my cell if you need me to pick anything up for you. Love, R." The note is scrawled in Rachael's near illegible handwriting, but after a year of dating and more than a year of living together, he's mastered her chicken scratch.

Damn! He'd forgotten all about Grammie's birthday party on Saturday. The thought of the party puts a damper on his morning. Joe comes from an enormous Italian family, and at every family gathering, he's subjected to the same tiresome round of questioning: "When are you going to propose to that beautiful girl and make an honest woman of her?" At least a dozen older aunts and uncles chime in to grill him on the topic. Not one to mince words, Grammie is usually the worst offender: "What's a matta wid you, Joseph?" she demands. "Stop your livin' in sin and marry that girl!"

All nagging ancient relatives aside, why doesn't Joe marry Rachael? At 33, she's every bit as hot as she was the day he met her. With her dark, wavy hair, deep-set green eyes, and petite yet curvy figure, she's a real head turner. His younger brother never misses an opportunity to tell him what a nice "rack" she has. If that weren't sufficient, she's got the brains to match her beauty; she works at one of the top architecture firms in the city. Then, why not make it official? Ask Joe that question, and he'll say, "*Why* make it official? We already live like husband and wife. Why go through the hassle of buying a ring and planning a wedding? It's a lot of brouhaha for a piece of paper, if you ask me!"

That's Joe's official answer. In order to fully understand Joe's "nonmatrimonial" mentality, let's jump into his head and reveal what he is really thinking but isn't prepared to talk about openly with Rachael. The deeper truth is that after actually living with Rachael, Joe is not convinced that she's the woman with whom he wants to spend the rest of his life. From the outset, he saw the whole cohabitation thing as a test run for marriage, and at this pit stop, he's not sure that Rachael has passed the test. When the two of them made the decision to shack up together, he thought that living under the same roof would be every bit as fantastic as their dating life had been. He thought he was signing up for continuous fun and mind-blowing sex. Alas, living with Rachael hasn't been the fun-filled sex romp he expected it to be. There are no more deep, meaningful talks or hysterical laugh fests. These days, their conversations are pretty mundane: What color should we paint the living room? Who's going to take the cat to the vet? Chinese takeout or pizza? Also, the sex has dwindled down to once or twice a week.

It's not that Joe is unhappy with Rachael or is thinking of breaking up with her. He has no desire to look for a new apartment right now or undertake the hassle of splitting up all the stuff they've bought together. He just isn't positive he wants to sign up for the lifetime package with her. For now, he's eminently content for things to stay just as they are.

• • • • • COHABITATION GONE WRONG • • • • •

It's fairly obvious that Joe and Rachael are in relationship limbo. How they got there is no mystery. Theirs is a clear-cut case of cohabitation gone wrong. Shacking up is a tricky business that, if handled incorrectly, can put the brakes on even the best of relationships. If Joe and Rachael never marry, they'll join the ranks of millions of other couples who made it over the threshold together but never to the altar. Just peruse these sobering stats:

- After five to seven years, 21 percent of cohabiting couples have yet to marry.
- The likelihood of a first marriage's ending in divorce after five years is 20 percent, while the likelihood of a couple's breaking up after cohabiting for five years is 49 percent.

Later in the chapter, we'll dish out some of the reasons that cohabiting couples never hop onto the marriage boat, but now I'd like to take a closer look at the last point, the fact that the likelihood of divorce is higher for couples who live together before marriage. Herewith are the reasons researchers believe this occurs:

- Folks who are willing to cohabit are often the same folks who are more divorce prone to begin with. These folks might be less committed to "traditional family values" and more skittish toward long-term relationships.

Certain attitudes and behaviors that develop during cohabitation may set a marriage up for failure. For example, living with someone might establish the precedent that the purpose of a relationship is to test a couple's compatibility. If, after marriage, it turns out the two begin to have problems getting along, they might be quicker to end the marriage, with the assumption that it failed the compatibility test.

The final reason for the increase in divorce among cohabiters is that couples who cohabit find it much more difficult to break up, according to *The National Marriage Project*. Within this process, a couple living together who might otherwise have called it quits might stay together and ultimately drift toward the altar and into marriage.

Regardless of all the liabilities, cohabitation is here to stay. Once reserved only for those on the fringes, it is now viewed by society as an entirely acceptable life choice. Some people even think of cohabitation as a substitute for marriage. While this viewpoint is all well and good, here's where things get complicated: if your ultimate goal is to marry a man, moving in with him might destroy your chances of making that happen. There's no need to pout in pondering that pronouncement, since there is a way to move in with a man and preserve your chances of marrying at a later date. In this chapter, in addition to probing the possible pitfalls of cohabitation, we'll roll out the secrets to moving in to marry. The same assurance holds if you're already shacking up, because we're also going to enlighten you about how to salvage your chance of making it to the altar.

•••••• THE PERILS OF SHACKING UP ••••••

 Today's couples move in together for many different reasons. Some do it to save money—most likely they're spending all of their time together anyway, so why not pay one rent together instead of two rents separately? Some shack up because it's convenient. Take my friend Julia as an example. Julia started seeing Brandon, they fell in love, and about a year into the relationship his lease ran out. As fate would have it, Julia's roommate was getting married around the same time. Brandon needed a place to live, and Julia needed a roommate. Perfect! Next thing you know, Julia's trying to make room in her apartment for an ice hockey table, and Brandon's trying to make peace with two cats and the color pink. Other couples decide to cohabit because they want to take their relationship to another level, but while they feel ready to sign a lease together, they're not quite ready to sign up for a lifetime together. Still others see cohabitation as a way to try each other on to determine if marriage would be a good fit.

In theory, each of these reasons seems plausible, especially the last one. With such a high divorce rate in our country, it

WHY I ASKED HER . . .

It was not lust or paralyzing physical attraction, nor was it the standard cliché "She will be a great wife and a great mother of my children," and certainly it was not financial stability. It was far and away the hours that we spent on the phone talking about any and every subject. It was about the friendship that we developed and continuously grew. I never held back a thought or behaved anyway different from how I normally am. No, we are not completely identical, nor are we total opposites—just compatible. I consider our unity just like a big jigsaw puzzle—all different pieces fitting together to be a picture that we consider beautiful. In life, every moment is an experience. When I realized that there was no experience I wanted to have without sharing it with Dianna, I asked her to be my wife. Oh yeah . . . she is hot, too!

—*Mike, married to Dianna for fifteen years*

does seem foolish to marry someone without having lived together first to judge if you're compatible. After all, you wouldn't buy a pair of shoes without first trying them on. All things being equal, each and every one of these reasons is legit. That is, unless the person with whom you're planning to share a bathroom also happens to be the man with whom you want to walk down the aisle. In other words, becoming his housemate could throw a hefty wrench into your plans of becoming his life mate.

Here are the three most common ways that cohabitation can put the kibosh on your wedding plans:

1. **She assumes his wanting to live with her means he eventually wants to marry her.** Wrong! One major misconception many women have about shacking up is that if a man wants to live with you, then that must mean that he ultimately wants to marry you. This, ladies, is not the name of that tune. Many men have completely different standards for their cohabitation partners versus their future marriage partners. When the mission is choosing a marriage partner, their criteria are much tougher. For instance, he might put up with a woman whose sex drive is lower than his in a cohabitation situation in which he's mainly just looking for companionship and help with the bills, but when he addresses himself to choosing his future wife, her enjoying sex as much as he does is a must.

Bottom line: assume nothing. If he says the two of you should move in together to save money, don't assume he means "to save money for our future together as husband and wife." Hear what is being said: he wants you to live with him to save money. A future wedding date was not implied. A woman might imply something instead of saying it outright, but what a man says is what he means. That's not because we're more honest than you are; it's because we flat-out don't have the ability to communicate in the complex way that you can.

2. **They decide to live together first as a test-drive before marriage.** This is a big mistake many couples make. Men, especially, often view cohabitation as a way to test-drive a relationship before deciding to marry. Yes, we try on a pair of shoes and take a car for a test run before deciding whether to buy. What we don't do is try on those shoes after they have been schlepping through the mean streets of New York City for five years and have a hole in the sole. And we don't test-drive a car after it's just hit a gigantic pothole that's sent its alignment all out of whack. When we try on that pair of shoes and test-drive that car, they're all new and shiny. Life is full of challenges, and there's not one of us who's all new and shiny at the end of every single day! With the commitment of marriage, men and women are much more likely to muster the resolve to hang in there through the bad, boring, annoying, frustrating times as well as the sparkly, shiny times.

3. **Cohabitation complacency sets in.** After living together for a while, couples get so caught up in the everyday demands of their lives that they allow the relationship to fall by the wayside. If you're dating someone but not living with him, and you both begin to ignore your relationship—you stop calling, you stop planning dates, you stop texting or e-mailing—then the relationship ends. Simple as that. In counterpoint, living with someone allows you to have your cake even if you don't eat a single slice. You can stop putting thought and energy into the relationship and not necessarily lose the person, because you're both on the lease and you share a bed.

Unfortunately, cohabitation complacency is commonplace. Some people believe that once they move in with someone, they no longer have to work on the relationship; they believe they can just put it on autopilot. They stop planning outings together, she stops getting decked out in sexy lingerie, and he stops leaving her romantic little notes and giving her compliments. They become more like roommates than lovers. (This also happens in marriages, but that's another book.)

Whatever you put your energy into grows—and vice versa. If you stop putting energy into your relationship, it's going to end whether you live with the other person or not. I know couples, and perhaps you do as well, who live together even though the relationship is dead as a doornail. They continue to cohabit because their lives have become tightly entangled—everything they own they bought together, and each has become part of the other's family and social circle. To me, this is a sad state of affairs. Having romance in your life is important and can enrich your existence in too many ways to even count.

• • • • • • • • • • MOVE IN TO MARRY • • • • • • • • • •

 Now that Matt has given you insight into what can go wrong if you move in with your significant other without an engagement ring on your finger, I'm going to inform you how you can move in with him without dashing your hopes of marrying him. I'm going

TOP TEN REASONS *NOT* TO MOVE IN TOGETHER

1. You want to save money on rent.

2. Your roommate is moving out, and his lease just ran out.

3. You hate living alone.

4. You feel it will move you closer to marriage.

5. You are moving to the city where he lives, and it just makes sense.

6. You want to keep tabs on him.

7. All your friends are doing it.

8. There will be more sex.

9. It's a great way to tick off your parents.

10. He's better than most of the guys you've dated, so what the hell.

to begin by telling you about the experience of a good friend of mine. Her name is Stephanie, and we go way back—all the way back to our frog-kissing days.

Stephanie is a tall, blonde bombshell. She's one of those women whom you look at and think, "She could have any man she wanted." Maybe so, but even though Steph is also warm, fun loving, and adventurous, whenever men entered the scene, she was always superguarded. This reserve in combination with her beauty ended up intimidating most men. Add to all this the fact that she was an artist and spent most of her days cooped up in her studio painting, so she didn't meet many people in the daily course of her life. It wasn't unusual for her to go long stretches without a single date.

Then one night she met Sam at an art exhibit, and he asked her out. They immediately clicked. It happened that they had a ton in common. It didn't hurt that the guy was a total winner, either. He was smart, kind, funny, adventurous, handsome, and responsible; he was everything she had ever wanted in a man and more. It wasn't long before they became serious. After about a year Sam asked her to move in with him. Taken off guard by his offer, she told him she would have to think about it. Stephanie is an extremely thoughtful person; she thinks things over carefully, and she thinks about things deeply. After weighing his offer for a week or so, she invited him to her place for dinner. Over the meal she basically told him that she was in love with him but that she didn't need a roommate. She didn't need someone with whom to share bills and chores. She told him she was perfectly happy with her living situation and her life, so why would she give all of that up to move in with him?

Sam quickly apologized for not having been clear. He told her that what he meant when he asked her to move in with him was that he wanted to begin the process of meshing their lives together, a process that he ultimately wanted to seal with marriage. Stephanie, being the smart cookie that she is, then asked him when he saw them officially sealing the deal. He said, one year. In so many words she said, sign me up!

I wanted to share Stephanie's story with you because, in my opinion, she totally rocked the cohabitation negotiations. If you're in talks with your boyfriend about possibly moving in together, and you want to move in to marry, here's the best way to go about it:

1. **Have the cohabitation conversation.** This is the conversation in which you tell him what moving in together means to you and find out what it means to him. First, some talking tips: Give him a heads-up that what you are about to say is important. This way he'll have a chance to get into the necessary frame of mind to process the message. Also, be direct. Don't back into the discussion by asking, "How do you feel about me?" or "Where do you see our relationship going?" You're there to tell him how *you* feel about him and where *you* want the relationship to go.

Once you have his attention, tell him that you will live with him *only* as a precursor to marriage, not as a trial run before deciding whether you want to get married at some later date. Feel free to use Stephanie's tactic—which wasn't a ruse, by the way; she was happy in her life and had built a lovely home for herself. Tell him you aren't looking for a roommate but do want a life mate. If he responds that he isn't ready for that level of commitment, that means the two of you are not on the same page. You know that he is the man you want to marry, but he isn't confident that you are the woman he wants to marry. Or maybe he isn't sure marriage is for him. If he's on the bubble, then you must remember that moving in with him is more likely to sway him against marrying you than convince him that he does indeed want to pledge you his troth.

2. **Set a deadline.** If after you tell him your stance on living together, he tells you that he's on the same page and that he views cohabitation as a step toward marriage, then you must ask him for a time frame. His response cannot be vague; he can't say, "In a few years" or "When the recession is over." You need a specific deadline with which to work, such as a year or two years from now.

3. **Set ground rules.** If his calendar matches yours, then the next item on your agenda is to lay some ground rules. You're reading this book; he isn't, so you're fully aware of the dangers of cohabitation. While you have his attention, tell him in plain English that moving in with him does not mean you want to stop dating him. Tell him your expectation is that you will both continue to put as much thought and energy into the relationship as you currently do, maybe even more. Maybe even, if you like the idea, suggest that you two set aside at least one night a week for a good, old-fashioned date night. And ladies: say all of this, and mean it! Be prepared on your end to continue to work on yourself and the relationship and to hold him to the same standard.

• • • • • • • • • • • • COHAB REHAB • • • • • • • • • • • •

 Follow the three steps Tamsen has laid out for you before you move in with him, and I guarantee you'll avoid the cohabitation pitfalls that so many couples encounter. So far, so good, but what if you've already fallen into one of those ruts? What if you've lived together for three years, and he still hasn't asked you to marry him, or you're both already suffering from a bad case of cohabitation complacency? If this is how it went down, there's still a chance you can pull him and yourself out by checking your relationship into cohab rehab.

Self-Help

The first round of therapy in cohab rehab involves looking in the mirror and administering a little self-help. The school of thought here is that you can't control a damn thing he does, but you can control everything you do! Consider the following:

☐ **Mirror, mirror on the wall.** Are you taking care of yourself physically? Are you keeping up your appearance, or since moving in with him have you put on a few pounds and stopped shaving your legs? Have you stopped wearing all the cute, little come-hither outfits you used to don for him and now taken to walking around in your comfy sweats 24-7? If so, knock it off!

Of course he's not asking you to marry him; you're a mess! Get back to the gym, and start wearing makeup, doing your hair, and dressing cute again. You have to get yourself together, girl—not just for him, but for your own benefit. Remember, when you looked hot, guess what: you felt hot, too!

☐ **Girls still wanna have fun.** Are you taking care of yourself emotionally? Have you stopped hanging out with friends and making an effort to have a social life, because, well, why bother, since you have a guaranteed companion waiting for you on the sofa at home? If you answered yes to that question, knock it off! Get back to nurturing your other relationships and interests. No one wants to marry a total bore who doesn't have a life!

Relationship Intervention

Once you realize what steps you need to take to get back on the right track, give yourself a time frame—say, six months—to get the new you up and running. Once you're feeling wonderful about yourself and you've got your social life cranking again, a relationship intervention is in order. This intervention comes in the form of a "post-cohab" conversation with him.

Follow all of the talking points Tamsen gave you for the "cohabitation conversation," with one additional rule: start off the conversation on a positive note, so he won't go into defensive mode. Don't say anything to the effect of, "It's time for

WHY I ASKED HER . . .

It became clear to me that I really had no choice. Without her at my side, anything and everything meant significantly less. I also started to consider her in every decision in my life automatically. I started to think about my life as having two parts: before I met her and after I met her. Interestingly enough, the second part of my life (with her) became much more important.

—*Paul, married to Aretha for twenty-one years*

you to stop taking me for granted, mister! I've been cooking you dinner every night for three years, and what do I have to *show* for it? Do you see a *ring* on this finger?" Instead, start off something like this: "Baby, I really love living with you; it's so awesome to come home to you every night, but now I'm ready to take our relationship to the next level. It's time we talked about marriage."

Don't be afraid to bring up the "M" word. If he's on the same page, he'll most likely be relieved that you broached the topic and saved him the trouble—unlike you, he's good with tools, not words. But do be prepared for him not to be on the same page. If you want to get married and he doesn't, your next move is to reevaluate your relationship and your living arrangement. Though you may be reluctant, the timing couldn't be better, because now you're looking totally hot and feeling great about yourself, and you've got your bustling social life to help you through the trauma of a breakup. At the end of the day, you have to be true to yourself and what you want out of life and not settle for less. You deserve the best, lady!

Cohabitation is a trend that's settled in for the long term. It's become a popular stage in the journey a relationship takes. We've endeavored to give you the orientation you need to decide if it's a stop you want to make on your own relationship journey. If you conclude that it is, take our advice to make sure it's not the end of the ride, but just another milestone along the way.

EXTINGUISH
HIS FEARS OF
WEDDING HELL

"Are you kidding me? I've been planning my dream wedding since I was 5 years old! As soon as Kevin pops the question—and hopefully it'll be soon—I'll be ready to get the show on the road," says Meghan, who is chatting on the phone with one of her best girlfriends. Her friend eagerly asks for all of the details of Meghan's "dream wedding."

"Well," Meghan begins, thrilled to get the opportunity to gush about her favorite topic, "I have my heart set on an Irish-themed wedding. My wedding colors will be kelly green and gold. Each of my seven bridesmaids' dresses will be a different color of the rainbow, with me as the human pot of gold at the end! No, no, my dress isn't gold; it's white, but it'll have a lovely gold sash around the waist, and my earrings and shoes will be gold. Kevin and all of his groomsmen will wear kelly green vests and gold ties with teeny shamrocks on them.

"Plus, we'll hire a professional mixologist to concoct a one-of-a-kind cocktail just for our reception: the 'Kevin Loves Meghan Martini'! And of course, the open bar will be fully stocked with Guinness. Also, there'll be plenty of Irish music on the band's playlist. As for the logistics, the ceremony will be held at St. Patrick's Cathedral—of course! And the reception will be at the Central Park Boat House. And instead of a wedding cake, all of the guests will get their very own miniature two-tiered cake decorated with a shamrock on top!

"Plus, and this is one of the things I'm the most excited about, we're going to hire a choreographer to design a first dance for us that reflects our personalities! Isn't that *awesome?* For only $1,500 they teach you a dance and give you a video of the rehearsal! I'm thinking the song we'll dance to should be Sinatra's 'New York, New York,' since that's where we met and fell in love. . . ."

Fade out and cut to Kevin. At the moment, he's standing stock-still outside of Meghan's slightly opened bedroom door. Unbeknownst to Meghan, her roommate had let him in. Kevin didn't mean to get caught in an eavesdropping situation; he was just about to enter Meghan's room and surprise her, when he heard the words "as soon as Kevin pops the question." This stopped him in his tracks. If you look closer at Kevin, a 34-year-old investment banker originally from Chicago, you'll see that he's pretty good-looking. He's tall and lean, with an athletic build. Kevin's been in a serious relationship with Meghan for about a year and a half now. It hadn't taken him long to fall hard for Meghan, who's 27. It was not just because of her stunning good looks—she's a tall, thin blonde with the figure of a swimsuit model—but also because of her outgoing personality and delightful sense of humor.

Right now, however, he isn't thinking about Meghan's good looks or her sense of humor. After the bit about the choreographed dance lesson, his brain switched into panic mode, and the only thought it's registering is: "Run!" He would, but as with a cornered animal, he has no place to go. Meghan's roommate is blocking his exit out of the apartment, and on the other side of the door in front of him is a potential bridezilla discussing her master plan to humiliate him in front of the world. Luckily, at this point, his overloaded brain has stopped working properly, so he's spared most of the details of the rest of the conversation. All he hears is: "Blah, blah, blah, flowers . . . photographer . . . invitations, personalized CD . . . wedding favors . . . four-course dinner . . . blah, blah, blah."

Finally, the torturous phone call ends. For the rest of the night, he's completely out of it. He tells Meghan he thinks he's coming down with the flu and goes home instead of staying over, resisting her efforts to play nurse. Once he's alone, his poor brain attempts to process what it's heard. One thought keeps making it to the forefront of his mind: "Who the hell does she expect to *pay* for this Irish extravaganza? Me! That's who! I could put a down payment on a Park Avenue apartment with what that wedding would cost!"

Kevin is right. He's the only one with the means to pay for any wedding the two of them might ultimately have. Meghan is an actress and not exactly what you would call a working actress. Nothing much ever materialized from her "big break" three years ago when she played the body double of the then Hollywood "it" girl. Mostly she just goes to acting classes and works as a temp. Moving on, neither his nor her parents are in a financial position to pay for a wedding, especially not the wedding Meghan has in mind. By process of elimination, if there ever is a wedding (and right now that's a very big *if*!), he'll be footing the bill.

That night Kevin dreams he is standing in front of an ATM, entering his secret code. Frank Sinatra is using the ATM next to his. Suddenly gold coins begin spilling out of the machine and piling up around him. As he tries to stop the hemorrhaging of money, out of nowhere Meghan and seven scary leprechauns appear (along with his fifth-grade math teacher) and begin scooping the coins up with gigantic Guinness mugs. He shoots up in bed covered in a cold sweat. Meghan's dream wedding has become Kevin's nightmare!

• • • • • • • • • **THE WEDDING WILLIES** • • • • • • • •

 Kevin should be afraid. He should be very afraid. Today the whole wedding thing has spun out of control. Back in the day, weddings were small, intimate affairs. Would you believe that in the late 1930s, one-third of all brides had no engagement rings, receptions,

or honeymoons? How the times have changed! In the current millennium, the average wedding costs $28,704, and the average wedding guest list has 161 people on it. In the past, couples would invite close friends and family to witness their nuptials. Maybe there would be a small get-together afterward at which punch was served and congratulations were handed 'round. Today close friends, family, family of friends, friends of friends, and virtual strangers are cordially invited to attend over-the-top spectacles at which the focus is not on the union of two people in love, but on all that money can buy. It's clear that with a wedding industry that exceeds $161 billion in the United States alone, money can buy a lot.

With this new materialism has come a new objective: weddings have become less about marking the specialness of the occasion and more about putting on a good show and pleasing the crowd. And it's a tough crowd to please. I can't tell you how many people I've heard criticize a wedding they've attended—the bridesmaids' dresses were hideous, the cake was dry, the band was awful, the food was too spicy. Most likely you've been guilty of this yourself. Somehow, somewhere along the way—and I'm guessing advertisers and the media deserve a good portion of the credit for this—planning a wedding became a competition. The future Mr. and Mrs. Smiths are constantly trying to one-up the future Mr. and Mrs. Joneses.

Now, I'm no wedding basher. As you've been informed, Tamsen and I had a beautiful wedding, but it was a wedding that was within our means, and planning it in no way over-

WHY I ASKED HER . . .

It would be easy to say I proposed to my wife for all of her fantastic qualities (beauty, intellect, sensitivity, and strong values), yet it was much simpler than that. Deep down it was simply an inherent desire to be with her forever."

—*Cristan, married to Jennifer for seven years*

shadowed our focus on the commitment we were about to make to one another. (Super Tamsen planned the whole thing in about a month in the back of a news van.) What distresses me the most about weddings today is that couples aren't focusing on their upcoming marriages; instead they're putting all their energy into planning their "big day," but what about the rest of their "days"? Once the party ends, they don't know what to do with each other. Seven years later the marriage is over, and they're in divorce court.

Here's the clincher: because of the insane expectations that women and society now have of weddings, many unmarried guys, including guys in serious relationships, don't want anything to do with them. Either these guys make the conscious decision that the only way out of becoming the clown at their own wedding circus is to never propose to a woman, or the thought of having to participate in a wedding has made them so hesitant to propose that they've reached a stage of inaction.

Why hasn't he proposed? Well, it might be that he wants nothing to do with your dream wedding. It's a bitter pill to swallow, but many men flat-out hate weddings. Want some proof? About three years ago a website cropped up online at ihateweddings.com; every day thousands of men flock to the site, leaving behind many of their own indisputably valid reasons for hating weddings. The picture may look grim, but don't agonize if you're stuck in relationship limbo because your guy's a wedding hater. Tamsen and I have some advice for you on how you can put his wedding fears to rest and get him willingly to the altar.

HERE COMES THE BRIDEZILLA

Before Tamsen gives you some valuable input on what you can do to convince him that by proposing he's not buying a ticket to Wedding World, I want to give you a better understanding of how men feel about weddings. "Why should I care?" you ask. "After all," you point out, "I'm going to be the bride! It's my special day, not his!" Whoa, don't get all bridezilla on me. It's that kind of thinking that lies at the heart of the problem. It is his special day as well. I know you've been dreaming about your wedding day since you were a little girl. Meanwhile, he's been dreaming about pitching for the Yankees—or Red Sox, Cardinals, or whatever his team is—since he was a kid, but that doesn't entitle him to a position on the roster. You might be the one who's been fantasizing about the day, but that doesn't mean he shouldn't get to help set the tone and make the decisions. Tragically, thus far, men have had no say in how wedding traditions have been shaped. Take it from me that if men had had any say, there'd be a new sheriff in town:

- No wedding would ever be scheduled on a day when an important sports event is taking place—that leaves about a two-week window each year for weddings.
- The "reception" would be referred to as the "afterparty" and would be held at the best watering hole in town.
- Brides wouldn't wear those long, flowy gowns with veils; they'd be in minidresses with their cleavage spilling over.

Instead you gals have gotten to call all the shots. As a result, there's nothing guylike about weddings whatsoever. It shouldn't be a huge surprise, therefore, that many men hate them. While a dyed-in-the-wool wedding hater might be crazy in love with the woman he's with, he'll do what it takes to avoid having to write his heartfelt vows and recite them to her in front of two hundred people; strike all manner of humiliating poses that will go down in posterity in an album that costs as much as a flat-screen TV; pick out China, flower arrangements, or a style of calligraphy; or dance with her to a sappy song in front of a crowd of people, most of whom he doesn't even know!

One unsettling new development in the evolution of weddings that has men even less inclined to take part in them is

WHY I ASKED HER . . .

It was never my plan to be married. My parents went through a bad divorce. But when I met Alicia, I felt safe and successful, and I truly missed her whenever I was away from her. The day I proposed was scary, but I have never been the same man since. She is now the mother of our son but, first and foremost, my wife and best friend.

—*Martin, married to Alicia for seven and a half years*

that the tradition of the bride's father paying for the wedding is no longer the norm. Today, since many couples are waiting longer to get married, by the time they're ready to walk down the aisle, they're making more money than their parents. Also, many families simply can't afford to pay for the lavish nuptials their daughters want. So, now that guys are expected to pay for the thing they despise instead of just having to take part in it, many aren't even putting themselves in the position where this is a possibility.

To put it plainly: they're not proposing. And thanks to a perfect storm that was set in motion three decades ago, they don't have to. Today an unmarried man can have all the benefits of marriage—the woman he loves under the same roof as him and having sex with him without society's holding it against him. If by now you've come to suspect that your Mr. Right is not slipping a ring on your finger because he's afraid it'll awaken the bridezilla within, seize on Tamsen's advice in the next section, which will go a long way toward putting an end to his fears.

•••••• END HIS WEDDING WORRIES ••••••

 OK, ladies, you now have a handle on how the fear of the wedding could stop him from taking a walk with you down the aisle. If you are willing to forgo your dream of having that big blowout wedding, or if having a big wedding has never been important to you, or if you get the wedding willies yourself, then I have some advice that will help you put his wedding fears to rest.

▢ **Avoid "wedding porn."** Never leave "wedding porn" lying around where he can see it. If he's a wedding hater, he'll most definitely get jittery if he sees any bridal magazines or other wedding pornography in his midst.

▢ **Weddings are kryptonite.** Keep it together at other couples' weddings. I've been to a million weddings. As soon as the bride appears at the back of the aisle, I gaze, coo, and cry, and before I tied the knot myself, I'd imagine my big day the entire time. To a wedding hater, all weddings are like kryptonite. Instead of melting into tears at the sign of a bride, pull yourself together. Enjoy your friends' special occasions; don't spend the whole time thinking about yours, and if you do, keep it to yourself.

⊿ **Be easy . . . going.** Use a wedding experience, whether it be a TV show or a friend's wedding, to make it clear that all that wedding jazz is not for you. Don't launch into a big discussion; be brief and to the point, and then zip it. Maybe say something like: "People are getting totally carried away with their weddings these days. I'm all about keeping it cheap and sweet." Then breezily change the subject.

⊿ **Don't be a bellowing bridesmaid.** Don't get upset every time a wedding invitation comes in and make the passive-aggressive point that you're tired of being in the audience and ready to be front and center at the altar. By the same token, don't be sullen and moody when the two of you are at the wedding of a friend or family member.

⊿ **Keep her wedding to yourself.** Don't talk to him about other people's weddings. He doesn't want to know that your coworker is doing this, that, or the other for her wedding. Weddings are an interesting topic for us girls, but listen up: whether a guy is a wedding hater or is ambivalent about them, he doesn't want to talk to you about weddings any more than he wants to talk to you about your cycle.

Now here are a few tip-offs that your guy has a classic case of the wedding willies:

⬜ Every time he receives a wedding invitation, he outwardly cringes.

⬜ He thinks of a million excuses not to attend weddings to which he's invited.

⬜ If you are able to drag him to said weddings, he rails about what a waste of money they are.

⬜ When asked to be a groomsman or best man in a friend's or relative's wedding, he complains endlessly about it.

⬜ He says anything to the effect of "I hate weddings."

As you can see, it's not terribly difficult to discern if you have a wedding hater on your hands. I wasn't trying to state the obvious; my intention was to make you realize that oftentimes, the men in our lives do tell us who they are and what they're thinking. We girls just often suffer from selective hearing.

If your guy hasn't shown any outward angst toward weddings, but you have a feeling he might be internalizing his wedding hatred, you may figure: why not just ask him outright? In fact, you may be wondering why I don't advocate that you simply talk to him about his stance on the wedding issue in general. *Don't do it!* It's true that I'm a firm believer in communication, but it's not a good idea to talk about the wedding before you've had the marriage conversation. It would be like talking about in which hospital you plan to give birth before you even talk about where you both stand on having children.

Also, if you're a wedding girl, and it turns out he's a wedding hater, don't be dismayed. There's no rule that by default the wedding hater always gets his way, while you must resign yourself to a trip to the nearest justice of the peace. Not at all! When the time comes, there will be ample opportunity to share your feelings and hopefully reach a compromise with which you're both comfortable. Be of good cheer, because when it's time to have that discussion, you'll be able to bring a newfound sensitivity to the table. You now realize that the day belongs to you both. But, if you're in the preproposal stage (that's where most readers of this book likely are) and believe he might be hesitant to pop the question because of his anti-wedding stance, it's smart to take the advice I have given you to quell his fears, so he can go about the business of buying that ring.

In a way, all those wedding haters out there, whether they're men or women, are actually performing a role in bringing a bit of renewed perspective to our wedding-crazed society. Whenever a trend moves too far toward one extreme, it usually takes the development of a countertrend to bring things back into balance. It might sound as if Matt and I are wedding trashers, but we beg to differ. If a big wedding extravaganza is what both parties are equally up for, and it's something a couple can afford, I say go for it! But when we see a couple, as we often do, spending what would amount to a down payment on a house for a wedding and then going back to a rental apartment when the honeymoon is over, it makes us think their big day is taking precedence over their life together. To us, this is the real issue and the one we hope you'll take to heart after reading this chapter.

Realizing he might be hesitant to ask you to marry him because of his desire to avoid getting caught up in a wedding whirlwind will require you to reassess if you are a girl who wants a big wedding. Here's the issue as I see it: what's more important to you, marrying him and spending a lifetime together or living the dream for one day?

INDEPENDENTLY
YOURS

 Remember the very beginning of your relationship when you and your guy couldn't get enough of each other? You saw each other every chance you got, stayed up all hours of the night talking and having sex, and called in sick to work so you could spend an entire weekday together. *You* even blew off your girlfriends and the yoga classes for which you'd paid a small fortune just to spend even more time with him. When you weren't with him, all you did was think about him or talk about him with your best girlfriends. If the feelings were mutual, you can bet he was doing the same thing on his end—minus the talking about you with his best guy friends.

While the two of you were in the throes of romantic love, as unromantic as it's going to sound, you were as hooked on one another as a drug addict is on his or her substance of

WHY I ASKED HER . . .

I waited until my midforties to get married, because I could never find someone who didn't try to change to please me. When I met Whitney, she always looked beautiful, but natural. She didn't try to impress me with her career, and she always was in a good mood and brought me up when I was down or worried. She is the same person I married eleven years ago, and I love her for it.

—*Andrew, married to Whitney for eleven years*

choice. I hate to be the one to break it to you, but the butterflies and sweaty palms of new love have nothing to do with the excitement of finding a soul mate and everything to do with a sudden downpour of chemicals drenching our poor, addled brains—specifically, dopamine, which also happens to play a major role in drug addiction. So, when you felt intoxicated in the presence of your new love, in a way, you were. This addiction you had for your new love was a perfectly normal state to be in at that early stage in your relationship.

Now comes the big buzz kill: if the relationship is to have any potential of making it for the long haul, once the initial stages of romantic love play out and the mad chemical rush starts to taper off—as typically occurs within about six months—it's time for a bit of detoxing. It's at that point that the woman must get back to the business of living her own life and being her own person. Henceforward in the relationship, if she wants it to last, she has to continue to assert her independence. This is an important watershed, because if she stays stuck on him and becomes what we refer to as a "gluestick" girlfriend, the relationship is doomed.

In this chapter, Tamsen and I are going to brief you on the importance of holding on to your sense of self. By maintaining your independence, you will successfully nip two of the common fears he has of marriage in the bud: his fear of a settled, boring married life and his fear of the marriage's ending up a miserable failure in which you'll slink away with an armload of his hard-earned cash. Our hope is that you'll take something else away from this chapter. We hope you'll also come to understand how holding on to and nurturing your sense of self will ultimately make your life a fuller and happier one.

• • • • • • • • • • • UNSTUCK ON HIM • • • • • • • • • • •

We all know her. She's the girl who, when you ask her to hang out, has to discuss it with her boyfriend first. "Let me check with [insert poor schmuck's name here] first to see what we have planned" is her typical response to your invites. Which brings me to her next identifying trait: she never asserts her independence when she speaks. Instead of "I," it's always "We." "We love that restaurant." "We hardly ever do anything on Friday nights." "We don't watch 'Curb Your Enthusiasm.' " If she does tear herself away from his side long enough to hang out with you, she's either calling or texting him every half hour and constantly eyeing her cell to see if he's tried to reach her. She's a "glue-stick" girlfriend, all right, and she's a total bore!

How does her boyfriend feel about her clinginess? He most likely hates it! When Matt and I interview male clients, one of the questions we ask them is why they broke up with their previous girlfriends. Common responses are that she was "too needy," "too clingy," or "too boring." You might be saying as you read this, "Thank goodness that doesn't describe me! I'm not that girl at all!" Don't fool yourself, lady. You might not be as blatant about it as the woman I profiled, but there's lit-tle doubt you're guilty of not holding on tight enough to your own identity and of thereby losing at least part of yourself in your relationship.

It's common for women to lose themselves in their rela-tionships. Of course, this happens to men, too, but they're not reading this book, and there's no getting around the truth that it happens to us girls more. Think about it: women tend to be the more giving partners in their relationships, and often-times, that means giving up their identities. Whatever the rea-son, if you're too wrapped up in your guy or your relationship in general, you're not spending enough time nurturing your-self. If this is the case, his fear that the marriage will end up a miserable failure and you'll both end up in divorce court, where you'll abscond with half his stuff, isn't that unfounded.

Here's why: If you're not working on yourself, and your happiness is now dependent on your boyfriend, the odds are high that if you marry him, the marriage will indeed fail miserably. As an adjunct, if you haven't been focused on your own career and your own finances, can you blame him for seeing you as a potential drain on his?

It's time to stop being stuck on him and become stuck on you. If you want him to want to marry you, you must first make sure you're marriage material. Once you're on track to becoming the best you that you can be, any fear he might have about the marriage's ending in disaster will be off your shoulders. The following sections cover key areas on which I recommend that you focus.

Nurture Your Circle of Friends

If you're devoting so much of yourself to your relationship that you've neglected your friendships or put a moratorium on any efforts to nurture new friendships, you've done yourself a huge disservice. Our friends are food for our souls. They are the small number of other human beings on the planet who let us into their hearts, which in turn allows us to learn more about ourselves and the world around us.

Women, especially, need their girl friends. As already mentioned, women and men communicate differently. Therefore, when you're in the mood to have a true gabfest—you know: the ones in which you talk about the latest beauty regimen and reminisce about your childhood—fat chance your boyfriend is going to oblige. Your BFF, on the other hand, will be only too eager to chat about your plans for your hair or what kinds of clothes are best for your body type. On a more serious level, there are certain things we experience as women that only another woman can understand. That's not to say your guy friends aren't important too. I have always had platonic guy friends, and they're a blast! It's not cool to let them fall by the wayside either.

So, if you've been neglecting your buds, it's time to suck it up and make it up to them one by one. Also, don't ever stop opening yourself up to making new friends; your world gets a little bigger with every friend you make. Don't become the girl who all of sudden falls out of touch with her friends because she gets a boyfriend. One of my best friends did this every time she fell in love. She would meet a man and spend countless hours on the phone with me analyzing his every look, word, and move, and then as soon as she felt secure in the relationship, she would dump me for a while. I always knew when the relationship was about to end, because she would suddenly spring up again and ask me to help in the analysis of the breakup.

Be Career Minded

If you've allowed your career goals to get off track because you've been too wrapped up in your guy and your dreams of becoming his wife and the mother of his children, your solemn duty is to focus that energy back where it will benefit you the most—on your own dreams of achieving whatever it is you want to achieve in your professional life. I believe having a satisfying career is one of the most rewarding life experiences you can have. It rocks to kick ass in the workplace! Having a fulfilling career has been, and always will be, one of the most meaningful parts of my life.

If you are in agreement, you can skip to the next heading, but if you don't have any career aspirations at this juncture in your life, or if you disagree with me about the importance of having a satisfying career, then take what I'm about to say to heart: in this day and age, you can't depend on a guy to support you; you have to support yourself! Chew on this nugget: for the first time ever, a larger percentage of women are unmarried than are married. So, you may as well support yourself by doing something you love or at least enjoy. Spend some time focusing on what that something might be, and I promise you it will be the best time investment you've ever made. If you are still convinced that your future Prince Charming will pay the bills, keep in mind that even if you do get married, we live in a time when most households need two incomes, so again, why not do something you truly like to pay your share of the bills?

Money, Money, Money!

Women who are irresponsible with their finances terrify men. The reason why is pretty simple: they're afraid you're going to be a drain on their bank accounts. Also, when they think of marrying a money flake, they're reminded of Eddie Murphy's story about how his ex-wife took "Half!" (We'll talk more about marriage and money matters in Chapter 8.)

On the flip side, a woman who has her finances in order is a total turn-on for a guy. Here's why: guys are biologically wired to be providers. Back in the day, that required going out with a spear and bringing home meat. Today that translates to going out and getting a good job and making a good living. Plus, for better or worse, society looks to the amount a man earns when sizing him up, imposing that added pressure to earn a decent living. Therefore, men put a lot of stock in money (pun intended). If they see that you are savvy with your dough, it's a quality they appreciate. It's like sports. Have you ever observed how excited a man gets when he meets a woman who knows sports? All of a sudden he sees her in a whole different light. He can bond with her on that level. It's the same exact thing with money.

Looks Do Matter

Men are visual creatures. This is not news to you. I'm willing to guess that when you were on the dating scene, taking care of your appearance was a priority. You spent untold time and money on your hair, clothes, nails, and wardrobe. You kept your legs smooth and your eyebrows plucked. Not content to stop there, you went to the gym, did yoga, and kept everything nice and toned. Then it happened: you met your soul mate, became "comfortable" with him, and started letting yourself go. If I guessed right, get ready for a makeover, sister!

To begin, let's get physical. Get back in shape! You know what you have to do; if you're the slightest bit out of shape, you've already expended a lot of brainpower thinking about what it will take to get back to your fighting weight. Now do it! On top of that, do something cute with your hair; start wearing makeup and cute, sexy outfits around him again; and shave your legs and groom any other region that needs grooming.

Guys freak when their girlfriends stop paying attention to their appearance. Maybe that attitude is not politically correct, and I'm not inclined to condone superficiality in any form. What I condone is facing the cold, hard facts. One of my best guy friends recently confided in me that his three-year relationship ended because he was no longer attracted to his girlfriend after she gained fifty pounds. And this guy is no jerk; he's one of the good guys. Nor can he be considered an exception, in that every single guy who comes to us looking for a match lists attractiveness among the top qualities that are important to him in a woman.

Once again, I'm not telling you anything you don't already know here. If you want your relationship to last and to thrive, don't pull a bait-and-switch on him. The woman with whom he fell in love was cute, smelled nice, dressed sexy, and looked well put-together. He has no intention of going to the altar with a much larger, rounder, out-of-shape, unkempt version of that woman.

It's a Wide, Wide World

The world is a fascinating place; there are sights to see, books to read, people to meet, hobbies to try, movies to watch, food to taste. If you train all of your energy on your boyfriend and your relationship and don't expend any on exploring the world around you, you are wasting your life. We happen to live in one of the few places in the world where we are free to pursue our interests. Don't squander that blessing because you can't extract yourself from a guy. You are genetically and environmentally predisposed to have your own interests. Our interests are an important part of who we are as individuals. Some of us are drawn to art, some to travel, some to books, some to cooking, some to writing, some to decorating, some to Eastern medicine, some to yoga, some to fishing. Whatever your interests are, cultivate them. They're an integral component of what makes you you. Also, they make *you* more interesting.

If He Likes a "Gluestick" Girlfriend

I've talked about what you should be doing to maintain your identity, as well as how doing so can make you the best person you can be and in turn take his fear of a disastrous marriage to you off your shoulders. But what if he wants you to be *dependent* on him? What if he resents any time you want to spend apart from him or doesn't like it when you pursue your own interests? Here's what: head for the door! This guy is controlling and insecure, and if you marry him, chances are you will be sacrificing your own identity and independence. Most likely, you'd be in store for a lifetime of stifling misery.

• • • • • • • • • • • • DON'T BE A DUD • • • • • • • • • • • •

 Tamsen has given you the lowdown on how being a strong, independent woman will help convince him that you're marriage material, not to mention the other rewards: a happier, fuller, more joyful life. Now I'm going to plumb another of his big fears and explain how a strong, independent you can quash it. The fear I'm talking about is his concern that getting married will be a one-way ticket to a humdrum, boring life and that he'll lose the edge he has as the "unmarried guy."

I'd first like to give you a primer on what it means to be the "unmarried guy"—or the UG, for short. When you're the UG, whether at work, in the fantasy-football league, out with the guys on a Friday night, or even at the poker table, you're a star! You get extra points just by virtue of the fact that you don't have a wife waiting for you at home. This applies even if you have a serious girlfriend. Married guys perceive you as having a kind of freedom that they no longer possess. It's not a weird "guy thing," either. This is a perception that's perpetuated by society. Think of the related metaphors: you marry your girlfriend, and she becomes "the old ball and chain," someone who "keeps you on a short leash."

Fanning the flames for the UG are the many television shows and movies that depict marriage as the epitome of domestic doom. Kids are screaming, the wife is nagging, and minivans abound. To further validate this already sorry vision he has of marriage are the actual couples he knows up close and personal who are living the marriage nightmare. What with all that, can you blame him for not wanting to opt in?

How can you convince your own UG that to marry *you* is to set off on a lifetime full of fun and excitement? Here are a few suggestions:

- When you're both exposed to a situation in which marriage comes across as being a total drag, say something to the effect of, "What a bore! That is not going to be me when I get married!" Then zip it and quickly move on to the next topic. You're planting a seed here; you're not digging in for a heart-to-heart discussion of marriage.
- Whenever possible, avoid hanging out with boring married couples. Continuing the logic, if you know couples who are happily married and fun to be with, hang out with them whenever possible.
- Most important, don't be a dud. Tap into your adventurous side. Get in the habit of planning fun, exciting adventures for the two of you. Not only will this show him how upbeat

life with you can be, but also it'll reignite those initial sparks that you both felt in the early days of your relationship. Again, flash back to those early days, when the two of you couldn't get enough of each other, and all of your racing thoughts were focused on him. You were in what is known as either the "infatuation" or "romantic love" stage. As noted at the beginning of the chapter, during those six to eight months, your brain becomes literally awash with chemicals, similar to an adrenaline rush. In addition to dopamine, which makes you feel good all over and gives you that delicious glow, there is phenylethylamine. Often dubbed "the love molecule," phenylethylamine is the one that causes a racing pulse, heavy breathing, and heady emotions. (Chocolate is rich in this chemical.)

Unfortunately, or fortunately depending on whom you ask, the rush of infatuation wears off. Our brains simply can't handle being in such a state forever. The infatuation stage of the relationship gradually morphs into a calmer, more intimate stage. The chemicals that preside over this stage are created by endorphins and bring about a restfulness and stability. Luckily, these chemicals are addictive, which is one explanation for why couples stay married.

The thrust of this chemistry lesson is that researchers have found that when couples share new and exciting experiences—anything from a trip to Europe to a hike at a local forest preserve—their brains pump out dopamine, the same chemical that had you love-crazed at the beginning of your relationship.

A weekend river-rafting trip or even a drive to a nearby town to sample a new restaurant can light a spark in your relationship. Running with that thought and making these adventures regular can convince him that life with you could never gather moss.

While you're at it, encourage him to do things with his buddies, and you do the same. Make nights out with the girls a regular thing. Also, try to plan travel without him, taking occasional trips either with friends or alone. Guess what happens when you're separated from the one you love: more dopamine!

All of these steps will not only convince him that life with you could never be dull even with a marriage license but also help you both to nurture your independent selves, so that when you do come together, you'll each have so much more to bring to the table. That way you'll be helping each other to grow and evolve, not to mention it'll just make life so much more fun!

 WHY I ASKED HER . . .

She was the first woman who could make me laugh hysterically in the middle of a fight and completely forget what the argument was about. She was the one woman with whom I started each day knowing any bad experiences were forgiven and in the past.

—*Stephen, married to Mary for eight years*

TRICKS FOR A SEX-CESSFUL MARRIAGE

"Do you take this woman to be your lawfully wedded wife? To love her, honor her, cherish her, and have sex with *no one else but her* as long as you both shall live?" This might not be the way the question is phrased, but I guarantee this is how it computes in the male brain. Basically, the groom is well aware that by saying, "I do," he's saying, "I won't." That is, "I won't be able to have sex with another woman besides my wife for as long as I live." For many unmarried men today, the thought of making this promise is exactly what's keeping them from the altar.

Men love sex. That's not to say that women don't. It's just that men and women love sex differently. The female sex drive takes a different road from a male's. (This is a broad generalization, and it certainly doesn't apply to every woman, but it does to most.) For a woman it's more about what's between her ears; for a man it's pretty much about what's between his legs. I can't speak for women, but for us guys, it goes something like this: see the attractive woman; have sex with the attractive woman; go to sleep.

Our society is set up to celebrate the male sex drive, and our media inundate us with attractive women and with the message "Opportunities for your sexual gratification are everywhere, so why limit yourself to just one woman for the rest of your life?" For the most part this is a bold-faced lie—most men are lucky that any woman wants to spend an hour with them, let alone a lifetime. Nevertheless, this is the message that guys receive, and it's at the heart of the fear many men have of making a lifelong commitment to just one woman. To them, it's like being given the option of choosing only one piece of candy or an entire candy store, even though—unless he's in the small percentage of the male population consisting of rock stars, movie stars, royalty, and billionaires—the candy store is located only in his head.

Now here's the good news: contrary to popular belief, men are not biologically wired to have sex with more than one woman. Actually, it's just the opposite. Biologically speaking, for men and for women, the monogamy question boils down to whatever is the best method for ensuring that our genes are spread to the next generation. Because men have no idea when a woman is most fertile, a man has a better chance of getting a woman pregnant if he has sex with one woman than if he tries his luck with many women. Believe it or not, it's the female of our species who has more to gain from having multiple sex

WHY I ASKED HER . . .

I will be honest: I realized I had to marry her when her mind started to turn me on just as much as her body. It sort of freaked me out when her dinner conversation became as hot as our bedroom experiences.

—*Jason, married to Marianna for four years*

partners. Do the math: if a woman spreads her luck between the guy with whom she's in a "monogamous" relationship and a few other guys on the side, she has a better chance of getting pregnant. While men may be encouraged by society to seek out multiple sources of sexual gratification, their biological wiring is geared more toward monogamy.

This proves there's hope for those guys who are afraid to settle down with only one woman for a lifetime. The catch is that hope isn't exactly what you need if you want to convince the guy you're with at this very moment that marriage won't mean the end of an exciting and satisfying sex life. What you need to do is send your guy the message that having sex with you and you alone for the rest of his days would be akin to winning the sexual lottery. To help you get this message through to him, Tamsen and I have put together a bag of tricks that are guaranteed to show your man that you're all about excitement, adventure, and variety when sex rolls around. After all, while you might be just one piece of candy, there's no reason why you can't have an endless number of flavors.

•••• ANY NIGHT CAN BE HALLOWEEN ••••

 Your guy has been inundated by countless images of sexy women from the day he took a peek at his first skin mag. With that grounding, it's only natural that variety is a total turn-on for him. He's seen images of sexy women of all shapes and sizes, and he's developed a taste for diversity. Yes, he thinks you're totally hot, and he loves to have sex with you. He'd also like to have sex with a cheerleader some nights or a sexy schoolgirl on other nights, or maybe even his freshman-year science teacher, the one who used to wear those really tight sweaters.

Why not make his fantasies come true with you? It's no secret that you like to dress up. How many times has he waited for you to change from your sweatpants to your elegant evening wear? And what a transformation! It's as if you went into the bathroom as one woman and came out as another. Why not apply that same technique to transforming yourself from his girlfriend to his hot nurse? And if you want him in scrubs so you can have sex with a hot doctor? Why not? Two can play that game.

•••••••• ASSUME THE POSITIONS ••••••••

If you've been together for a spell, it's easy to get into a routine in the bedroom. You both lead busy lives, and just as you've worked out the best morning routine that gets you from your bed to your office, after a while you work out a surefire routine between the sheets to get each other from first base to home plate. While there's nothing wrong with that, it's imperative to strike a balance between old faithful positions and a willingness to try out the countless other fun and satisfying positions that are possible—even ones you never thought were possible.

There are more ways to get from first to home than you ever imagined. One way to explore a new position is to figure out what feels good organically. Another way is to simply get a book or an instructional video. Good books from which to choose are the tried and true: Alex Comfort's *The Joy of Sex*; a new take on a golden oldie: Anne Hooper's *Kama Sutra for 21st Century Lovers*; and one destined to become a classic: *101 Sex Positions: Steamy New Positions from Mild to Wild* by Samantha Taylor. If you really want to mix it up, you can buy a fun card deck of different positions, such as Dawn Harper's *Sex Deck: Playful Positions to Spice Up Your Love Life*. "Picking a card" has never been so exciting.

• • • • • • • • • BE A BABE IN TOYLAND • • • • • • • • •

Playing with toys is always fun. Playing with sex toys can take fun to a whole new plane. A platonic female friend of mine once described her first trip to a "sex shop." She said that based on the various offerings of that particular establishment, she was convinced that sex toys were designed and manufactured by male elves only. She—and you—will be pleased to know that the sex toy industry has finally caught on that women are important customers, and no matter how much *she* loves *him*, she's not letting him bring *that* anywhere near her if she doesn't like it.

Enter babeland.com, a website run by women for women who are looking for the hottest gadgets designed with women in mind. (If you want to double your shopping pleasure, another nifty site geared toward selling sex toys to women that I recommend is libida.com.) Babeland is not just a virtual sex shop. The website is the online version of two brick-and-mortar locations. Both the standing locations and the Internet presence pride themselves on customer service. They're run by a staff of "babes" who are there to answer your every question. The site is full of information, including advice on how to pick out the best vibrator, a list of handy "how-tos," and helpful sex toy tips. If you've always wanted to own the Vibratex Rabbit vibrator made famous on "Sex and the City," make tracks to babeland.com. Just don't forget to share your toys with your boyfriend!

• • • • • • • • • • • • • LEARN A SKILL • • • • • • • • • • • •

During our research for the book, we chatted with countless men and women for this chapter. One of our interviewees told us that after an operation, she was unable to have sex with her boyfriend for several months. She knew how important sex was to him, and she herself didn't want to give up the intimacy that came with being sexual with each other. So, she decided that in the interim, she would simply resort to giving him oral sex. In the past, giving her boyfriend oral sex had been just a prelude to intercourse; it wasn't an act she typically did for its own sake.

After the first week of oral-sex-only sex, she realized how unskilled she was at the whole thing. Then and there, she made the commitment to become a pro. After much research, trial and error, and practice (her boyfriend was more than happy to be her guinea pig), she said, she became a master at oral sex. Not one to rest on her laurels, she continues to add new tricks to her bag of techniques all the time. As for her boyfriend, he's a happy guy. It's no wonder: men love receiving oral sex. This is not something you've never heard before. Nevertheless, during our research, I was taken aback by how many of the married men and women to whom we spoke told me that they are not having any oral sex.

Ladies, if you want to crush your man's soul, stop giving him oral sex. If you want to blow his mind, become skilled at it. To help you develop proficiency at this particular job, there are some excellent videos, books, and even classes that will teach you the trusted techniques. Besides giving oral sex, another new skill you could learn that is custom-made to rock his world is the art of the striptease. These days, studios such as S-Factor teach women how to be expert strippers in the bedroom, and more such studios are cropping up all over the country. If taking a class isn't your cup of tea, you can avail yourself of some fun DVDs that will teach you to become his personal stripper.

• • • • • • • • • • • PORN TO BE WILD • • • • • • • • • • •

For most of its history, porn was made for men and enjoyed by men. Because the majority of the content has been targeted to males over the years, women have historically found the ideologies, not to mention the wham-bam sex, portrayed in adult videos objectionable. However, as with the sex toy industry, the porn industry has finally realized that if its targets its product to women, they will come. As a result, more and more women are seeking out and finding porn that's tailored to their tastes.

Men love porn. Once again, I've told you something you already know. Moreover, many men want to watch pornographic movies with their partners. This too is no shocker. But here's something that might give you pause (or maybe not): now many women like porn too. According to a survey by Janet Lever, a sociology professor at California State University of Los Angeles (CSLA), 41 percent of women in the United States have viewed or downloaded erotic films or photos. So, here's my recommendation: find a few adult DVDs that you like, and watch them with your boyfriend. If you have always been against adult movies, you'll most likely revise your attitude after watching a movie made with your likes, dislikes, and desires in mind. In our research, the adult film *Chemistry* came up time and again as a video that is popular with female audiences. It's a documentary about real people, not actors, who actually have sex with each other because they want to.

For more information on porn geared toward women, get your hands on *The Smart Girl's Guide to Porn* by Violet Blue, an author and the sex columnist for the *San Francisco Chronicle*. She's also written for the likes of *O* magazine and the *Wall Street Journal*. To further broaden your horizons, you can pore through the handy lists of porn made for women on both Violet Blue's website at tinynibbles.com and babeland.com. Just a little note: Even though it's considered "porn for women," it's way OK for men, too. Believe me when I tell you these are chick flicks he won't mind watching with you.

FABULOUS YOU

Be confident in the bedroom. This is a tip that might sound like a no-brainer, but for many women it's the most difficult thing to do in a sexual relationship. This is tragic, because there is nothing sexier than a woman who is confident and comfort-

WHY I ASKED HER . . .

She was my biggest supporter in taking a job across the country and leaving her back East. It was the day she told me to take the job that I knew I did not want to live without her. I proposed two months after I left and haven't spent a night away from her since.

—Jerry, married to Anna for nine years

able in her own skin. We've lectured you on staying in shape, and that advice still holds. After all, research shows that the better shape you're in, the more you'll enjoy and be up for sex, but no one says you have to have a flawless body to please him in the bedroom.

Yes, guys are plenty superficial, but your guy wouldn't be with you if he didn't think you were a total hottie. It's healthy to remember that no one is flawless. Even the "flawless" images of women with which we are inundated aren't flawless; they're Photoshopped. You are hot. Remember that. Being sexy and hot is both an inside and an outside job. Love yourself, and worship your body by not obsessing over its every "flaw." Do this, and confidence will come. If you struggle with confidence, do some inner work and figure out why, and please do what needs to be done to get past the issue, primarily for yourself, but also because—and I can't say this enough—nothing is sexier than a confident woman!

•••••••••• FREAKY, FREAKY YOU ••••••••••

 Nearly as sexy to a man as a woman who is confident is a woman who is uninhibited. If you've been reading our suggestions and blushing through each one, saying to yourself, "I could never do that!" then you're missing the whole point of this chapter. The point is to be an adventurous lover who is willing to accompany your guy on the sexual adventure of a lifetime.

In the previous chapter, we expounded about how sharing new experiences with your mate can reignite the spark the two of you shared at the beginning of your relationship. That premise holds for your sex life as well. New adventures in the bedroom can jump-start your sex life like nothing else. If you're not willing to try new things because of shame or embarrassment, get over it! One way to do this is to talk to your girlfriends about it. You'll be surprised at how adventurous most are, and it might give you the courage to try new things. I'm not saying you should do anything that makes you uncomfortable. What I'm saying is you should first ask yourself why you're uncomfortable, and if the only answer you can come up with is that you're supposed to be uncomfortable, then kiss that particular inhibition good-bye, because it has nothing to do with you and has everything to do with society.

One of our interviewees was raised to be a good Catholic girl. "Guilt" was her middle name. As an upshot, when she started having sex with her first boyfriend, it was all about the missionary position and not much more. After a while *she* got bored with things and belted out some dirty talk. She said that when lightning didn't strike her down, it was as if a whole new world had opened up to her. She's been an adventurer in the bedroom ever since. So, it might be as easy as taking one small step such as throwing out a bit of dirty talk to get your mind to begin opening to the wide, wide world of sexual possibilities.

BEYOND THE BEDROOM

Make a point to get out of the bedroom and have sex against different backdrops. Try different rooms, or go camping and try it in nature. I'm not going to give you too many examples; I'm not looking to get anyone arrested. You know your environment best, and you know where you can and can't get away with having a quickie or even a not-so-quickie. Use your imagination, and always be on the lookout for new venues, because I'm telling you: sex outside of the bedroom, like sex on the beach or in a dressing room at the Gap, can sweep you away!

JUST DO IT

According to the University of Chicago's National Opinion Research Center, the average adult is having sex only sixty-one times a year. Don't be on the infrequent side of that spectrum. Couples who have happy, healthy relationships have sex way more than that. I'm not going to assign any numbers to exactly how much sex you should be having, but between you and your partner, you have to figure out the compromise that works for both of you. This might require one or the other of you to make a sacrifice, but if happiness is to ensue, this is what has to be done. Keep in mind that people who have regular sex are in better health, feel more connected, and are at a lower risk for depression. So, no matter how busy you and your guy get, always make time for sex.

WHAT A GIRL WANTS

No one knows what turns you on more than you. Spend time thinking about it, experiencing it, and rehearsing how to articulate it. Then tell him! Tell him the when, the where, the how, and the why. Don't be afraid that by giving him guidance, you'll be bruising his ego. Nothing makes him feel more like the man than pleasing you. Believe me: he wants to know. Men aren't born knowing how to please a woman; they learn, and no one is a better teacher than you. Your sexual satisfaction is every bit as important as his.

We hope you now have a better understanding of where his fears of monogamous matrimony are rooted. We also hope you're relieved to know you're not dealing with a situation in which the lifetime mate you choose is programmed to be unfaithful to you or to always wish he could be. To boot, now you know that variety in the bedroom is the key to a fantastic sex life and will not only ease his fears of a lifetime of monogamy but also make your relationship stronger, healthier, more intimate, and all-around more fun!

FOR YOUR BAG OF TRICKS

Books

- ☐ *The Joy of Sex* by Alex Comfort
- ☐ *Kama Sutra for 21st Century Lovers* by Anne Hooper
- ☐ *101 Sex Positions: Steamy New Positions from Mild to Wild* by Samantha Taylor
- ☐ *The Smart Girl's Guide to Porn* by Violet Blue
- ☐ *The Adventurous Couple's Guide to Sex Toys* by Violet Blue
- ☐ *Sex Deck: Playful Positions to Spice Up Your Love Life* by Dawn Harper

Online Resources for Intelligent Women (These smut-free sites are for gals with brains!)

- ☐ babeland.com
- ☐ tinynibbles.com
- ☐ libida.com

"Smart" Porn Made for Women (Your guy will be glued to *these* chick flicks!)

- *Chemistry* 1 and 2. These "reality porn" videos focus on female pleasure. Performers are filmed in a house over a weekend. Described as "authentic."
- Comstock Films' *Xana and Dax* and *Marie and Jack*. These documentary-style videos feature couples deeply in love who talk about how they met and sex. Viewers see real-life chemistry between a man and woman who really love each other.
- Jenna Jameson in *The Masseuse*. Jameson stars in this video with her then husband. Described as having high production values and centering on female pleasure.

Not Porn Ready (Opt instead for these sexy movies.)

- *The Lover*. Based on the Marguerite Duras novel, this steamy film has been described as tasteful soft-core porn.
- *Mississippi Masala*. This erotic and romantic film from director Mira Nair stars Sarita Choudhury and Denzel Washington as two lovers who cross racial boundaries in the Deep South.
- *Kama Sutra: A Tale of Love*. The on-screen version of India's famed how-to sex guide is a lush, and feminist-minded, fantasy.
- *The Unbearable Lightness of Being*. Hot sex plus Daniel Day-Lewis. 'Nuff said.

I TAKE THEE TO
BE MY WIFE, NOT
MY WARDEN

It's Saturday morning, the sun is shining, and the temperature is a cool sixty-five degrees. It's a perfect day to be out on the golf course. Shawn calls his best friend, James, to see if he's up for a few rounds. "Absolutely!" says James. "But first, let me check with Hannah." Hannah is James's wife of two years. "Sorry, dude. Hannah got pissed when I asked her. She's been asking me for weeks to clean out the garage. If I go play golf instead, I'll totally be in the doghouse, which I just got out of after I met some people after work for drinks last week." Disappointed, but not deterred, Shawn calls Kyle, another one of his buddies from back in the day. "Sorry, dude. I can't make it today. Jillian's been giving me a hard time about all the golf I've been playing.

She says we never do things together on the weekends. Today
we have plans to go shopping for a new duvet and sheets. The
sheets we have now don't have a high enough thread count."

Shawn can't believe what he's hearing. He lived with Kyle
before Kyle met and married Jillian three years ago. Back then,
the guy slept under an old sleeping bag on a mattress on the
floor! OK, on to plan C: Dave. Another old buddy, Dave has
a pretty weak game, but he's fun to hang out with. "Sorry,
man. I promised Yolanda that I would go to the farmers' mar-
ket with her." This from someone who once ate Tyson's fro-
zen chicken nuggets for dinner every night for a year. "Damn,"
Shawn groans, "these guys are totally whipped!" Shawn has
had enough with married dudes. He dials the number of a
coworker who is single, Tim. "Sure, man. Meet you on the
course in an hour!" After hanging up the phone, Shawn makes
a vow: "I am *never* getting married! There is no way I'm giving up my life to spend the rest of my weekends in Bed Bath &
Beyond and shopping for heirloom tomatoes!"

At one time or another, every guy has done as Shawn did:
rolled his eyes at his totally "whipped" buddies while swearing
to the high heavens that he'll never end up where they are. Lo
and behold, many of those guys are now effectively putting
their money where their mouths are. How are these protest-
ers hanging on to their independence? Quite simply, they're
staying as far away from the altar as possible, choosing instead
the untethered life of singlehood. What this stance has bred
is that today singlehood is viewed as an acceptable life choice,
not an unlucky curse. The fastest-growing population in the

United States today is singles. Tellingly, according to a recent article in *Psychology Today*, 40 percent of first-time home buyers are singles, and 42 percent of the workforce is single. And you better believe that a large chunk of these singles are men who have sworn off marriage forever for fear of losing their independence.

If your guy is in any way fearing for his independence in his relationship with you, be warned: he may very well make up his mind that he'd rather go it solo than officially take you on as his "old ball and chain." But don't worry, sister: ever faithful, Tamsen and I are here to help. First off, we're going to identify the behaviors on your end that may be suffocating him. Once we show you what you may be doing wrong, we'll show you how to reverse the behaviors and go about your relationship in a way that allows him to breathe and maintain his autonomy. After that, we're going show you how you can communicate to your guy that if he marries you, he gets to keep his independence and continue to pursue the things that he truly desires in life.

Before we get into why it's essential for your guy to maintain his independence, we're going to give you some insight into the two ways that women suffocate their significant others the most. One is by being clingy and needy, and the other is by being bossy and controlling.

How can a man know if his girlfriend will be a clingy/bossy wife? Easy as pie: if she acts that way before they're married, she'll act that way after they're married. Check out Tamsen's following rundown of the first of the bad behaviors.

• • • • • • • •   ARE YOU A CLING-ON?   • • • • • • • •

 To get a handle on your possible clingy character-
istics, let's start with a brief diagnostic test:

▢ Are you content to spend all your free time
with your guy?

▢ Do you give your guy grief every time he mentions doing
something without you, such as playing golf or poker with
his buddies?

▢ When he does manage to free himself from your tena-
cious grasp, are you at home waiting for him to "check
in," as opposed to engaging in an activity on your own
that you enjoy?

▢ Do you freak out if he doesn't constantly "check in" when
you're not together?

▢ Do you give him the cold shoulder after one of his outings
without you?

▢ Do you emotionally blackmail him into doing things with
you that he hates, such as shopping for linens, trolling
garage sales, or going to "chick flicks"? In other words, are
you turning your boyfriend into your best gal pal?

If this is you, then, sister, you need to do a bit of soul-
searching and then make some serious changes—that is, if you
want to marry the man you're with. First, let's talk about why
you're clinging on so tightly. It's fine if you enjoy your boyfriend's company, but more often than not, women are clingy

because they are insecure. Take a look at a letter we received from 27-year-old Marcy.

Dear Matt and Tamsen,

Last night my boyfriend of a little over a year told me I was the "clingiest woman" he has ever been with. He said that he really does love me, but he just can't stand my clingy and needy behavior toward him. He said that when we first started seeing each other, part of what attracted him to me was how interesting I was.

Before we started going out, I spent a lot of time on my photography. It's been months since I even touched my camera. Even though it hurt to hear, I honestly do appreciate my boyfriend's having the guts to communicate how he feels to me. Everything he says is true.

I believe I behave this way because I love Scott so much and am so afraid to lose him. When we're together, I feel more at ease and reassured that he's not going anywhere; plus, I can keep an eye on him and make sure some other girl isn't turning his head. But now I realize that what I'm doing to make sure I hold on to Scott is the very thing that is pushing him away from me. What should I do? Please help!

Love,

Marcy

This letter handily summarizes the major reasons that women cling to their men. They're seeking constant reassurance that the guy they're with is into them and isn't about to walk. There's often a trust issue involved as well—a desire to "keep an eye" on the guy to make sure he's not being lured away by someone smarter, wittier, prettier, and all the other potential "ers" that exist. As Marcy now recognizes, this behavior actually ends up pushing guys away. For one thing, they feel smothered. For another, they miss doing the stuff they enjoy— the stuff they've enjoyed for years before they even met their would-be soul mates. And they hate the hassle of "checking in" and the constant arguments every time they want to do something on their own. Typically, that clingy behavior causes their attraction to the woman to take a nosedive.

There's no denying it if you're culpable: the cling-on that you've become is a far cry from the interesting, free-spirited, self-assured woman with whom your man fell in love. On top of all of that, if you don't trust your man, then you have a serious problem. A relationship without trust is doomed. Here's the bottom line: if you are insecure in your relationship, clinging to your man is not the way to find the security you crave. The only—and I do mean the *only*—way for you to be secure in your relationship is to foster a sense of confidence within yourself. It's an inside job, sister! You've got to love yourself and believe in yourself. Clinging to your guy is self-sabotage. In the end, it will only drive him away from you.

For the record, if a guy actually likes a girl to stick her tentacles into him and hold on for dear life, that, my friend, is a billowing red flag! That means he has his own issues with insecurity. Now let me tell you something else: insecurity truly does bring out the worst in people. It underlies some of the most destructive human behavior there is, including many of the behaviors that cause marriages to fail, such as verbal and physical abuse, substance abuse, dishonesty, and infidelity. You're wise to steer clear of Mr. Insecure.

As for Ms. Insecure, you must say good-bye to her forever and say hello to Ms. Self-Assured. Let your guy have his space. Don't give him grief every time he wants to do something without you. In fact, encourage it. Then, while he's off doing his thing, you do yours. Think about what the single you used to like to do, and get to it! Concentrate on your own happiness and self-fulfillment, and stop worrying about what he's doing every minute of the day. The best relationships are the ones in which couples come together to share their full and happy lives.

Remember that you're not there to hold one another back; you're there to give each other the support that each needs to grab life by the horns and live it! An added benefit to allowing him his independence and holding on to yours is that you'll notice that when the two of you come together after doing your own things, you'll have so much to talk about. Your conversations, which were once centered mainly on what movie to rent or what restaurant to go to, will actually become interesting again.

WHY I ASKED HER . . .

I had always wanted to have children, but I was very nervous about making a commitment to a woman, since my parents went through a nasty divorce. Rose came from an incredible family, and they made me feel welcome from the start. Over time, I watched her with her nieces and nephews and noticed how she loved to take care of me. I asked her to marry me after two years. She was about to take a new job and move to a nearby city, and I knew that I didn't want to be away from her. It turned out to be the best question I ever asked.

—*Bradley, married to Rose for three years*

• • • • • YOU'RE NOT THE BOSS OF HIM • • • • •

 I have a buddy who can't make a move without asking his wife's permission first; not doing so gets him "into trouble." Does this dynamic sound familiar? It should, because it's the one every one of us had with our moms growing up. My friend and many other poor schmucks out there are married to what I call "mother-wives." You know these women. They're often referred to as "she who must be obeyed" and said to "wear the pants in the family." Do you resemble a mother-wife? For instance:

◻ Are you constantly nagging your man, making "suggestions" about what he should and shouldn't be doing?
"Baby, take it easy on the cream sauce; you know how it
gives you gas." "Honey, you really should give up your
subscription to *Maxim* and start reading *Time* instead."
"Two hundred dollars on sunglasses! No way you're buying those!" "The thermostat gets set on seventy-five
degrees around here, not seventy-one degrees!" "Did you
put enough detergent in the dishwasher? You have to fill it
up to the top, you know."

◻ Are you constantly bossing him, telling him exactly what
to do or not to do? You've got to clean that garage today!"
"You're coming with me to Macy's to pick out new tow-
els." "Las Vegas? For a bachelor party? Forget it!"

◻ Do you baby him? "Does my little shmoopie have a head-
ache? Aw, here, take two of these aspirins and hold this
cold compress on your forehead." "Here ya go, cupcake:
hold this thermometer under your tongue for three min-
utes. That's a good boy!" "Be sure to put sunscreen on
your neck! You know how you tend to burn there!"

Does any of this sound familiar? If so, lady, you've got to
kick the habit. If you treat him like a rebellious teenager, that's
exactly how he'll start acting. First, he'll start to resent you,
and then he'll begin to full-on rebel against you. He'll begin
doing things not because they're the right things to do, but
because he wants to show you that you're so not the boss of

him. As the sun sets, the sexy, hot woman he once saw you as will begin to morph in his mind into the shrill, bossy nag you've become. This is not cool. He was superattracted to the sexy, hot woman; the shrill, bossy nag—not so much. Worse yet, and this is backed by research, women lose sexual interest in men when they start becoming their caretakers. All in all, if you're constantly mothering your guy, you are thoroughly sabotaging the chemistry you have for each other.

If you are mothering your guy, you need to figure out why. Women behave this way in a relationship for two salient reasons. Sometimes only one reason applies in a situation, but other times, they operate in tandem.

Reason number one is control. Women with control issues want to be in charge, not only of the relationship but also of the other person in the relationship. Note that whether it's the woman in a relationship with control issues or the man, it's always a problem. Couples should always be working toward maintaining a fifty-fifty split in this regard. The relationship should run on communication and compromise; it shouldn't be a constant power struggle. Too often, two type A's end up together, and their relationship is an all-out battle. In one variation, the more easygoing type B puts up with the type-A control freak only until enough is enough, at which point the type B finally explodes.

Control in a relationship should always be fifty-fifty, with no partner ever trying to control the other. People are meant to be in charge of their own lives. If someone is so passive that he or she wants another to be in total charge, then that person

WHY I ASKED HER . . .

I asked her to marry be because she was the one from the moment I saw her. My friends thought that I was crazy and that my feelings for Kate would pass, but they only grew stronger. I believe in love at first sight and in soul mates. Kate is my soul mate, and I cannot imagine my life without her in it.

—Jamal, married to Kate for five years

has big-time issues. If your guy actually seems to relish the control you exert over him, this is a major red flag. You do not want to spend your life with a man who isn't taking responsibility for his own.

The second reason women resort to mothering their men is that they have a strong desire to change them. I once had a platonic female friend who was in love with a man. He was a brilliant classical musician, and she was drawn to his talent and genius, but in every other area of his life, the guy was a mess. He was a slob; his finances were always in disarray, because he couldn't remember to make deposits or pay bills; he slept all day and stayed up all night composing, paying little attention to his appearance. My friend was the opposite of this guy in every way. The two simply were not compatible; yet, my friend was determined to turn him into a man with whom she could get along. To no surprise, the relationship didn't work out.

The moral of this story is that you really can't change someone. While I stand by that statement, I don't subscribe to the old saying that people can't change. I believe that we all change; we grow and evolve throughout our lives. The distinction is that any change that does happen comes from within. It happens because we want it to, not because someone else wants it for us or for him- or herself in order to get along better with us. The conclusion to be drawn is that if you're mothering him in order to try to mold him into the person you want him to be, you must stop. It's not going to happen, and he'll only end up resenting you for your efforts.

OFF THE MENU: BARHOPPING/BOOZING

I hope you now realize the merits of giving your guy the space he needs to maintain his independence. With that matter thus settled, there is a bit of "single behavior" that he doesn't get to retain and on which you have every right to put your foot down: barhopping and boozing. If by "pursuing his own interests," he means going out clubbing every weekend with the boys and getting wasted, that's totally not OK. Your relationship must be built on respect. Heading off every weekend with the boys to clubs or bars, drinking too much, and staying out too late is disrespectful to you. Of course you're going to worry about what could happen when alcohol and the bar scene mix. You're only human! Let's lay another related detail on the line while we're at it, which is that "hooking up" is a large part of the club and bar scene. Regularly putting himself in a situation in which that kind of behavior goes with the territory is patently unfair to you.

I'm not saying that an occasional "boys' night out" or "girls' night out" should be off the menu. To the contrary: both should be encouraged, but the operative word is *occasional*. Further, in those situations, both parties must have their fun while always respecting the significant other. "Hooking up" is never an option. One technicality to keep in mind here is that going to a sports bar with the guys to watch a sporting event doesn't fall into the category of barhopping and boozing. It's a totally different scene, which is about male bonding and enjoying a televised competition with fellow fans.

· · · · · · · · · · · ·   **A BALANCING ACT**   · · · · · · · · · · · ·

 If we've done our job, you now perceive the importance of allowing your guy to maintain his independence and be his own person. That's not to imply that both of you shouldn't be putting your energy and time into doing things that are for the good of the relationship. Likewise, it certainly doesn't suggest that he should never compromise and do something that you want to do but that he's not necessarily into, and vice versa. It also doesn't mean that both of you shouldn't do your part to make sure the

household runs smoothly. What it does mean is that it's necessary to incorporate both his and your individual interests, desires, friendships, and goals on the list of priorities in your relationship.

Now then, how do you make it clear to him that his retaining his individuality is important to you after you marry? An effective way to get this point across is to comment on married couples, or even couples who are just in long-term relationships, who don't make this a priority in their relationships. Tell him how important you believe it is for both parties to maintain their autonomy in a relationship. Tell him with your words, *and* then show him with your actions.

IT'S ALL RELATIVE

The fact that you're reading this book suggests that you're in a relationship with the guy you're hoping eventually will ask you to be his wife. Further to that assumption, I'm going to draw the conclusion that you've entertained a daydream or 2 or 237 of your wedding day. I'm betting you've pictured how you will look all gussied up in your white dress and veil, holding a lovely bouquet of your favorite flowers. Wow! You make a breathtaking bride! I'm sure you've also envisioned how it will be to stand at the end of the aisle arm in arm with whoever will give you away on that special day. From that vantage point, you can see your beloved groom standing at the altar staring at you—overcome by your loveliness. Boy, he sure cleans up, doesn't he? What a dreamboat!

Now I want you to humor me a bit. Imagine your guy standing at the altar waiting for you, just as you have dozens of times before, only this time, instead of being flanked by a line of his closest buddies, arrayed next to him is a lineup of his closest family members. Can you picture it? There standing right next to him is his mother. She looks nice—but why is she looking at you with such disapproval? Now she's whispering something into his sister's ear. His sister is nodding in agreement. Want to know what they're talking about? His mother is saying that you should have taken her advice and worn your hair up instead of down, because you have a round face, and when you wear your hair that way, you look chubby. How rude!

Never mind them. Let's scan the rest of the family. There's his dad next to his sister. Wait a minute. What's he holding up to his ear? Is that a handheld *radio*? Can't he take one day off from *football*? Standing next to him is your soon-to-be brother-in-law. Well, he's not exactly standing; he's swaying, because he's completely wasted. Geez! It's only 2:00 P.M.! Oooh, he nearly knocked over Grandma! Poor Grandma. It looks as if her goiter's gotten much bigger since Thanksgiving. Granny might look rough, but not half as rough as your soon-to-be husband's kid sister. Couldn't she have covered up her tatts for the church service?

I believe I've made my point. Nevertheless, allow me to spell it out for you just for the sake of emphasis: when you take him to be your wedded husband, you get his family—and his close buddies, for that matter—as part of the package, for better or for worse. It's important for you to understand the magnitude of this situation, because the success or failure of all of these new relationships will have a great deal of influence on your future together. On the more immediate front, if you play your cards right while you're in the preproposal stage, your ability to get along swimmingly with his family and friends could help you land that proposal.

In this chapter, Tamsen and I will tutor you on how you can use the good graces of his family and friends to your advantage. As the lesson continues, we'll give you tips on how to successfully steer your way through your relationships with his family and close friends now and after you've become an official part of the picture.

• • • • • • • • • • • ALL IN THE FAMILY • • • • • • • • • • •

 If you're at the point in your relationship where you're thinking about marriage with your long-term boyfriend, chances are you're pretty well acquainted with his family already. Maybe you've even already spent a holiday or two with them. If his family members have embraced you with all of their hearts and are easy to get along with, count yourself as one of the lucky ones, because so often, this is not how that cookie crumbles. In addition, with the high divorce rates from the 1960s through the 1980s, odds are that he's a product of divorce and that you're entering the scene of an already tension-filled drama.

Whatever your level of interaction with his family, whether satisfying or otherwise, there's one fact on which you can rely: once you're married, it's going to change. That's because these assorted people will have higher expectations of you as his wife than they did of you as his girlfriend. You must do your best to get along with his family. In itself, your willingness to do so is one way that you can show your prospective husband how important he is to you. Also, your ability to establish loving ties with his family can only have a positive effect on your relationship. Turning it over to the soft underbelly, a contentious standoff between you and them can cause much stress and controversy in your relationship.

Establishing positive ties with your future in-laws isn't necessarily going to be an easy task. There's a reason the term *in-law* has a negative connotation, while the term *monster-in-law* can send shivers down a girl's spine. Viewed from even the most objective angle, the relationship between a woman and her in-laws has a couple of strikes against it from the get-go. Strike one is that you're an outsider being introduced into an already bonded group of people. Strike two, the relationship between a mother-in-law and a daughter-in-law comes with a built-in potential for discord, because both parties feel a similarly strong sense of possessiveness toward the same individual.

To help you manage your relationship with your in-laws, Matt and I have come up with a handful of tips that, if put into practice, will make for a peaceful coexistence. Take a look:

☐ **Show up for family functions.** The best way to get to know his family is to spend time with them. Don't be the girl who always thinks of excuses not to go to family functions. If the event is being held at a family member's house, score some extra points by calling beforehand and offering to bring something to help out.

☐ **Make an effort to fit in.** Every family has its own set of traditions and activities that help keep it bonded. Some families play charades when they get together; some play card games; others center their gatherings on cooking together and sharing a big meal. Similarly, all families have their own sets of holiday traditions that make the celebration unique for them. Be a good sport and always participate in the various traditions and activities of your prospective or newfound in-laws. Never sit in the background and have to be beseeched to join in. The best way to be accepted as part of the family is to act like part of the family. A friend of mine told me that whenever her boyfriend's family get together, they like to play Trivial Pursuit. So, the last time the family assembled, she made sure that she was the one who suggested they play the game. Even though this was a small gesture, she said it made her feel like a part of the family to be the ringleader of an activity that she knew everyone was looking forward to.

☐ **Be a friend.** Make an effort to get to know his family members as people. Just as you would with any potential new friend, have conversations with them about their careers, hobbies, and backgrounds. You're bound to have things in common with one or a few of them. Play up these common bonds. For instance, if you and his mother both love to cook, ask her for recipes, and talk to her about new cooking trends you've heard about. One of our clients told us that she and her boyfriend's kid brother are both loyal "Lost" fans. So, every time they see each other, they chat excitedly about the past episode or watch reruns together. It seems like a minor item over which to bond, but we're talking about a teenage boy and a 30-something grown woman; finding any common ground is a triumph!

☐ **Treat his family like A-listers.** It's a unique time to be a couple just starting a life together. It wasn't too long ago that most couples just starting out went from their parents' homes to the home they would share. Typically, the newlyweds' new digs weren't too far from the childhood homes they had just left behind. Perforce, their parents and immediate family were very much a part of their married lives. These days, many 20- and 30-somethings relocate to new cities and spend many years living on their own and enjoying the single life—a life that isn't as conducive to spending time with family as married life— before they decide to settle down and wed.

This being the case, often once a couple decides to get married, they have two robust social circles to merge together, which can leave little time for family functions. This is where consideration comes in. I know how busy you and your guy are with your bustling social lives, but make an effort to include your in-laws in your life. If you are lucky enough to develop a bond with your boyfriend's sister or mother, give her a call just to chat. If you live in the same area, be alert for fun things you can do together. Always remember birthdays and special occasions. And whenever you're together, go the extra mile to make his relatives feel special. Give them your undivided attention. Don't constantly be checking your e-mail or taking calls on your cell. Let them know in any way you can that they are on your A-list. This will be a giant step toward nabbing you a spot on theirs. Getting down to brass tacks, if his family members like you, they'll do everything in their power to get your guy to officially make you a part of their clan.

Allow him alone time with his family. Before you become a dues-paying member of the clan, your guy may feel a bit of pressure when the two of you are with his family. He wants to make sure that you're comfortable and that his dad isn't boring you with details of his last fishing trip, or that his brother isn't shocking you with talk of his new band's swarm of groupies, or that his mother isn't making you watch the videotape of his winning act in his third-grade talent show. For these reasons and others, every now and again, it's nice for him to spend time with his family without the added pressure of having you along. So, if he wants to go fishing with his dad or hang out with his brother without you, don't be offended. Quickly swallow your pride, and then encourage it as heartily as you can manage.

WHY I ASKED HER . . .

I knew she was the one when she refused my first proposal by telling me I hadn't quite mastered the art of "handling her" and to check back in six months. I did, and my second proposal was granted.

—*Chris, married to Natalie for three years*

Don't overshare. It's true that no one knows your guy's bad habits and quirks better than his immediate family. While it may therefore be tempting to seek commiseration from his mom or sis when you get into an argument with him, don't do it. Don't tell them about the set-to you had with him because he's been drinking too much or because he forgot your anniversary. Commit this to memory: nothing good can come from letting his family in on your relationship woes. If they side with you against him, you incur the risk of causing a rift between him and his family. Be cognizant that most people's relationships with their families are a minefield. You never know when one small rift can set off an explosion of years of pent-up hard feelings. Even if you and your guy end up kissing and making up, painting him as the bad guy with his family could land him in hot water with them. If this happens, he will inevitably resent you for your part in putting him there. Also, letting them in on your relationship problems will give them the idea that your relationship is their business, and once you open that door, it's impossible to close.

• • • • • • • • • • • FUTURE OUTLAWS • • • • • • • • • • •

Now you have a few surefire rules to follow to place you in the good graces of his kinfolk. But what if you've tried every trick in the book to get them to like and accept you, and they don't? Sometimes, through no fault of your own, your potential in-laws will dislike you. Even worse, sometimes they'll regularly let you know in no uncertain terms just how much they dislike you. The sad fact is that some people turn out to be wonderful human beings *despite* their families, not because of them. If your guy is one of those people, have no fear, because Tamsen and I also have prepared the following tutorial on how to deal with future "outlaws":

▢ **Present a united front.** It's to everyone's benefit that you make your boyfriend understand any problems you are having with his family. If his mother constantly puts you down, for instance, or his brother attacks you for your politics every time you're in his presence, make your boyfriend aware of what's going on. Explain to him why the situation is unacceptable to you. While his family is understandably important to him, he needs to realize that if you're going to spend your lives together, you must come first, and he must do his part to ensure that you are treated with respect by his family. Then figure out a plan for him to talk to the offending parties and set some boundaries regarding their behavior toward you. For example, if the problem is his mother's putting you down, he must make her aware of what she is doing and tell her that she must stop and that if she doesn't, she is jeopardizing her relationships with both of you.

Hit the eject button. You have no control over anyone else, but you do have complete control over yourself. If any of his family is behaving toward you in a way that you deem unacceptable, whether it's just one member or—worst-case scenario—the entire clan, don't hesitate to remove yourself from the premises. Do your best not to engage in any negative discourse. Without fuss, inform your boyfriend that it's time to leave, and then eject yourself from the situation. Your leaving will speak for itself. It will say, "I will not tolerate this behavior." Also, be sure your guy gets it across to his family that if they want you both to participate in their functions, they'll have to treat you with respect or carry on without either of you. Life is short; don't waste any of your precious time on this planet around people who, for whatever reason, want to tear you down.

Spare him the drama. Avoid making the problems you have with his family a prickly issue in your relationship. Don't remind him every chance you get that being among his family is impossible. Rest assured that he knows. Instead of letting his dysfunctional family come between you, use the situation as an opportunity to become even stronger allies. If his family can be somewhat on the nutty side, it's a reasonable assumption that growing up with that group has been difficult for him. This puts you on tap to be the one person on whom he can count to understand and help him overcome the challenges of having a dysfunctional family. Make it clear to him that if he ever wants to talk about it, you're ready to listen. Always do what you can to make this particular complication in his life less stressful. Most important of all, convey to him that the two of you together will break the cycle of dysfunction by being a healthy family unit unto yourselves.

Don't stir the pot. Especially when you know the hot spots, don't ever be the one to initiate an argument with a member of his family. For instance, if you know that his father is a staunch Republican, and you are a liberal Democrat, never bring up politics with him. You're in control of you, so do your part to keep the peace.

Forgive. No matter how rocky the initial interactions were with either one member of his family or all members of his family, never close the books on the possibility of reconciliation. If a family member who was once a sworn enemy extends the peace pipe, and it's a genuine gesture, always be willing to accept it.

In the domain of possible outlaws, you still have one more hurdle to clear. Ahem, his family may not be the problem— yours might be! It's a two-way street, and you must also consider how he will deal with his own set of potential outlaws. Here are a few suggestions for helping him embrace, or at least defend himself from, your family unit:

◻ **Have a family powwow.** While your parents no doubt are precious to you, you must nevertheless set some boundaries so that everyone understands each other. Trust me: if your mother knew her meddling was driving your man away, she would not be doing it. She likely is just trying to stay involved and demonstrate how much she cares about him and approves of him. Have a firm but gentle conversation with your folks, letting them know they will always be a part of your life and the life you are about to share with your future husband.

◻ **Have his back.** One of the worst things you can do, even if you flatly don't agree with him, is to side against him in front of your family. If there is an issue over which he and your family are at loggerheads, wait until you are alone to let him know exactly how you feel about it. Even if you have opposite stands, remaining loyal to him should take precedence.

◻ **Put your family in perspective for him.** Although it's a truism that he will actually be marrying the family if he marries you, don't make him think he is going to be sacrificing every chance at happiness to them. Let him know that you will spend time with your family but that none of them will be moving in and taking over his life as you proceed to build a future together.

 Stop being the cruise director. If your family and your man clearly don't get along, and your relatives are driving him batty, stop being the cruise director. You don't need to stage a show to cajole them to enjoy each other. If your mother and father are difficult for him to take in large doses, don't plan a three-day outing with the family. If you want to see your folks, maybe visit them without him sometimes and take him with you sometimes. Allow them to warm up to each other at their own pace.

Debrief him fully. He needs to be aware that your family's opinions are not yours. This means that after you have that fireside chat with your parents in which you are going to set boundaries, you must do the same thing with him. Instill in

---

WHY I ASKED HER . . .

Unlike other women, Melinda understood it was OK for me to be my own person. She gave me freedom, she never pressured me, and she was always my biggest supporter whether I was being promoted or being fired. I asked her to marry me because I knew that I wanted to have her by my side through the good and the bad.

—*Marc, married to Melinda for three years*

him that you love and respect your parents and would never do anything to hurt them but that they can be a little strange sometimes. Then be as specific as possible. Explain to him exactly what he's in for. The best thing you can do is make sure he knows he can come to you when he is having problems with them. He should also know that you are an individual and are not your parents.

·········· FRIENDLY PERSUASION ·········

Just as essential as cultivating a harmonious relationship with your boyfriend's family is making an effort to get along with his best buddies. I can't stress enough just how integral it is to be on good terms with his friends. In our business, Matt and I take pains to learn from both matches that work and the ones that don't. One way we do this is by keeping in contact with our clients. When a match works and turns into a relationship, we interview the clients to find out what went right. Similarly, when a match initially works but sours after a while and ends in a breakup, we elicit information on what went wrong. When we talk to men about successful matches, time and again we hear that the woman got along great with his friends. When we talk to our male clients about failed matches, we get the same feedback in reverse: she didn't click with his friends.

Like it or not, for many men, what his friends think of his girlfriend looms large. Men crave a measure of acceptance from their buddies when it comes to the women they choose to date. This being the case, you're wise to capitalize on it. I believe that making friends with his friends is an ideal way to make double sure that your guy realizes how special you are. While it's common knowledge that guys don't spend much time talking to each other about their relationships, read my lips: if his friends don't like you, they'll make sure he knows it. By the same token, if they like you, they'll get that across as well. Following is my time-tested advice on how to win over his friends. Once you implement it, you'll have trusty partisans in your cause of getting him to the altar.

⌐ **Encourage him to hang out with his friends.** If you want his friends to despise you, keep your guy from spending time with them, either by monopolizing his time or by pitching a fit whenever he wants to be with them. In the early part of your relationship when you're both totally hot for each other and want to spend every waking minute together, he'll easily be persuaded to stay in with you instead of hanging with his pals. Soon enough, though, once all those wacky new love chemicals have run their course, he'll see your efforts to keep him from being with his friends for what they are: insecurity and manipulation. If you want him to want to marry you, this is not how you want him to perceive you. Encouraging him to spend time with his friends will pay dividends all around.

⬜ **Get to know his friends.** When you're in a social situation with his friends, make an earnest effort to have meaningful conversations with them and get to know them as people. Show an interest in their lives and their interests. In turn, share details about yourself with them. If you follow this piece of advice, your guy's pals will see you as more than just his girl and will get to know you as the fabulous person you are.

⬜ **Don't play matchmaker.** Steer clear of trying to set up your girlfriends with his guy friends. Dollars to doughnuts, even if they hit it off at first, it won't work out in the long run. If it ends badly or even just awkwardly, you may find yourself stuck in the middle. You'll also expose yourself to the risk of ending up in a situation in which your guy's buddy forever associates you with a negative experience.

• • • • • • • • • • • • FRENEMIES • • • • • • • • • • • •

Now I'd like to address an all-too-common scenario in the context of significant others vis-à-vis friends: the situation in which your guy doesn't get along with the girls. If your friends and your soon-to-be fiancé are like oil and water, don't fall into the trap of taking sides or demanding that he get to know them and love them. Your task is to stay on course in your relationship with him and your relationships with your friends, who most likely were in your life way before he showed up. Here are some strategies that might help with this predicament:

⊿ **Don't force them on him.** Don't put him in a situation in which he is forced to be one on one with any friends of yours whom he doesn't like. Inviting a friend he dislikes to dinner with the two of you is a terrible idea. Either spend time with each separately or, if they do have to be together, make certain it's in a group setting. In time, he might actually grow to like this person. After all, you love them both, so there must be something special about each. In the meantime, either keep them apart or put them together only in light, group settings. Regardless of how the cold war progresses, he owes you the respect of always being kind to the people you love, whether he cottons to them or not.

⊿ **Allow his "boys" to be present.** It may sound a little juvenile, but the best way to make sure that he is comfortable around—or at least can tolerate—the friends of yours who rub him the wrong way is to urge him to invite some of his friends along for backup. This tactic may not always be feasible depending on the event or situation, but when it is, it's a good way to let him feel that there is an even playing field.

⊿ **Go it alone.** If he doesn't need to be there, then go out with your friends on your own. This is not only doing your guy a favor but also doing your friends a favor. While they may not always come clean about it, it's possible that they're not his biggest fans, either.

⊿ **Stop trying to sell him.** The less you try to "sell" him on your friends, the better off you will be. If there is any chance of his getting to know them personally and eventually warming up to them, it needs to happen organically. By talking up your friends, you make him feel as though you are trying to convince him that they are great. If they really are great, he will find it out on his own.

To recap this chapter, no man is an island. When you sign up for him, his family and posse are part and parcel. While you get to handpick the man you marry, your future in-laws are a crapshoot. If you're lucky, you'll win the in-law lottery and end up with a second family you'll be glad to call your own. If not, adhere to the advice we've given you, and you'll have minimal trouble taking on even the most disagreeable outlaw.

HANDLING YOUR POTENTIAL MONSTER-IN-LAW

❑ **When she tries to pry into your sex life.** Just as Charlotte did in "Sex and the City," stand your ground and be direct. If she asks about how often you have sex, answer her without an answer, such as: "Things are great all over. We enjoy each other immensely. You raised an amazing son." This will smoothly divert the conversation.

❑ **When she insists she knows what her son likes better than you do.** You must be respectful of his mother (it just comes with the territory), but you don't have to stand there like a Stepford wife. Say to her that you appreciate her input and will take it into consideration. Then, do with it whatever you want. Also, keep in mind that every now and then, she may know better than you, but it's up to you to decide if you need her two cents.

❏ **When she is critical of you.** First of all, don't let it get to you. Tell yourself that this is her problem, not yours. Second, don't think for a minute that just because she's his mother, you have to be her punching bag. It's OK to stick up for yourself.

❏ **When she fights for her son's attention.** This is one area that doesn't need much handling. Let her run and get him a second helping, fold his laundry, and laugh at the joke he can't stop repeating. Accept that he's her son, and they have a special bond. Be happy for him that he has a mother who loves him.

CHECK HIS BAGGAGE ... AND YOURS!

 In the previous chapters, we've walked you through the many steps *you* can take to get to the altar. In this chapter, we're taking the spotlight off you and shining it on *him*. We're less concerned here about turning you into a bride and more concerned with making sure the groom you so desperately want is the best man for you. Here's the thing: in our society, women tend to be more driven to marry than men are. As such, they're willing to push any concerns or misgivings they have about their relationships under the rug. The problem is that these issues don't stay hidden for long. After the "I dos" are exchanged and the honeymoon is over, they reemerge just in time to start chipping away at the marriage. Before long, the marriage, imperiled from the start, becomes just another divorce statistic. We don't want you to become another statistic.

We know that you love him, but we also know that love isn't enough. It takes so much more to make a successful marriage. What does it take exactly? Funny you should ask, because that's what we'll be disclosing in the following pages. We're even going to show you how the status of your current relationship can predict your odds for marital success. We'll also supply insights into what the experts—Tamsen and I included, of course—believe make a man marriage material. Will your guy measure up? Does he have what it takes to be your husband? Rounding out the topic, we're going to ask you to check his baggage against yours to see if they're a match. Do you both want children? Are the two of you financially compatible? Will religious differences impact your life together? Everything in this chapter is meant to help you determine if the guy you're hoping would pop the question is even altar worthy.

IS YOUR RELATIONSHIP "MARRIAGE MATERIAL"?

I know you've spent a lot of hours dreaming about your wedding, but how much time have you spent contemplating what marriage would actually be like with your nominated dream groom? If your answer is, "Not much," it's high time you get down to it. "I wouldn't know where to begin," you say. "It's not as if I can pull out my crystal ball and look into the future." Good point, but here's a better one: you have something at your disposal that will work way better than a crystal ball to predict what married life would be like with your groom-to-be. You have your current relationship, which can serve as a blueprint of your future marriage together.

Relationship researchers have found that certain characteristics of a premarriage relationship can predict whether a marriage will succeed or end in divorce court. On this topic, I defer to one of my favorite relationship gurus, Dr. John Gottman, a psychologist who has spent years researching marital stability and divorce prediction. He often speaks of four predictors of divorce. These four red flags are so accurate that the doctor has come to refer to them as the "four horsemen of the apocalypse." If your relationship bears any or all of these characteristics, it might be a good idea to stop imagining a trip down the aisle and start thinking about a trip to couples therapy.

☐ **Contempt.** Dr. Gottman has said that this characteristic alone is the most reliable predictor of divorce. So, if it's common for you or your guy to hurl direct insults at the other, be sarcastic with the other, or harbor an air of superiority toward the other, the gods of wedded bliss are not smiling down on you.

☐ **Criticism.** Constant criticism and put-downs also don't bode well for a happy union.

☐ **Defensiveness.** If either of you constantly responds to a complaint from the other by adopting the stance of an innocent victim or with an air of righteous indignation, this could be another sign that your relationship is not marriage material. According to Dr. Gottman, this behavior shows an unwillingness to take responsibility for problems.

☐ **Stonewalling.** If either of you tends to withdraw emotionally during a conflict or confrontation, the odds-on bet is that a marriage between the two of you wouldn't be a happy one. Ask yourself: Does your guy shut down all verbal and nonverbal communication during a conflict, opting instead to look away from you? Or, is this a tactic you yourself use during an argument?

Now that we've identified potential red flags in your relationship that can take the wind out of your marriage aspirations, let's home in on relationship traits that are signs that a couple will be able to withstand the pressures of married life. Because it's our business to know, Matt and I have done a heap of research in this area. We've learned much from what other experts have to say, but we've learned just as much from the many happy couples we've come across in our matchmaking/relationship coaching business. Here is a roster of relationship characteristics and behaviors that we believe can predict a successful marriage:

☐ **An ability to enjoy just hangin' with each other.** Members of couples destined for wedded bliss spend a lot of time laughing, joking, and goofing around when they're together. They find it easy to be with each other. They are each other's best buds and have just as much fun sitting on the sofa together on a Wednesday night channel surfing and eating ice cream as they do going out on the town together.

⊿ **A genuine sense of caring and concern for one another.** Another reliable indication that a relationship will last is that the partner's mental and physical well-being is just as important to each person as his or her own. The partners take care of one another when illness strikes and are there to lift each other's spirits in times of gloom. Because each wants the other to be happy, they are willing to make compromises when necessary.

⊿ **Keeping an open channel of communication.** Communication between men and women is no easy feat, but couples in solid pairings have figured it out. These individuals know how to talk to each other when something is on their minds. Equally as important, they know how to listen to one another. They don't keep their frustrations bottled up or show anger or hurt feelings by zipping up and doling out the silent treatment.

⊿ **"Getting" each other.** In couples with staying power, each person has a deep sense of understanding of what motivates the other and how the other's mind works. Each understands the other's hopes, fears, ambitions, humor, insecurities, flaws, passions, desires, and quirks, and they love each other because of them and despite them.

⊿ **Being truly interested in each other.** When members of successful couples ask how the other's day was, they really want to know. Each is legitimately interested in what the other's thoughts and opinions are on various issues, and they are continuously surprised and delighted by each other's growth and evolution as human beings.

⌐ **Knowing how to argue.** Disagreements are inevitable in a relationship. Couples who know how to argue in a way that is productive and directed toward a resolution have a leg up on making it for the long haul. These couples don't stoop to name-calling. They're not in it to hurt one another. Also, they stay on topic when they disagree, as opposed to bringing up events that took place five years ago on New Year's Eve.

⌐ **Sharing the same values.** This one is last, but I believe it's among the key predictors of marital success. The importance of sharing the same values is something I heard time and time again but never really understood until I met Matt. I always thought "sharing values" was more about having the same views on religion or politics. Now I realize that it means that you have the same priorities in life. For instance, here are some of the values Matt and I share: our families and friends are important to both of us; we both love helping people; we both are career oriented and enjoy work; and we both love living and working in New York City.

Researchers have also found that members of couples in marriages that are successful share similar levels of agreeableness and conscientiousness. Agreeableness is the tendency to be pleasant and accommodating in social situations. People who are considered agreeable are typically empathetic, friendly,

WHY I ASKED HER . . .

I believe I asked for all the right reasons, but I didn't know it at the time. I asked Sueanne to marry me after we had dated for three years in college. We had fun together, and we had the same set of values. But today I realize that it was much more than those things that has kept us together. We have grown together; we have shared both good and bad times, but we never go to bed angry and always remember that respect is the one thing you must have to make a marriage work: respect for yourself and for your soul mate, no matter how tough it gets.

—Adrian, married to Sueanne for fourteen years

considerate, and helpful. Those who are highly conscientious are careful, thorough, and self-disciplined; think carefully before they act; and are hardworking and reliable.

• • • • • • • • • WHAT IS HIS "I DO" IQ? • • • • • • • •

 Here's where we put your groom on the hot seat. Earlier in the book, we talked about whether you were "marriage material." Now it's time to think about whether your guy is the marrying kind. As a matchmaker, I've had access to hundreds of relationships. I've seen

the good, the bad, and the terrifying! As a result, I've honed the ability to tell when a guy isn't right for a woman. Although every case is individual, there is a test I've developed over the years to help clients figure out if their guy is marriage worthy. I call it the "I Do" IQ test. If it turns out he has a low "I Do" IQ, marrying him most likely would be a big mistake. Here are the test questions, along with the keys to how the answers determine his "I Do" IQ:

Does He Treat You with Respect?

People often use the word *respect*, but when asked for a definition, most are hard put to give one, because it's a word that is overloaded with meaning. When I talk about a man's having respect for his girlfriend or wife, what I mean is that he treats her in a way that shows that he has a high regard for her and that her feelings, happiness, opinions, and well-being mean the world to him. When a man respects a woman, he would never intentionally do anything to hurt her.

Sometimes the easiest way to understand this level of respect is to point out when it is absent. He isn't showing you respect if he does any of the following: insults you, criticizes you, lies to you, fails to ask for your input when making decisions that affect you both, displays a lack of courtesy and kindness to your family and friends, allows you to worry about him unnecessarily, breaks his word to you, or neglects to express gratitude for the things you do for him. If his behavior scores low on the respect-o-meter, you're not sitting pretty under that waving red flag.

How Does He Treat Others?

If he is wonderful to you, that's dandy. The caveat is that if he goes through the world treating others with contempt, unkindness, and inconsideration, you may well be his next target. If he's a jerk to the world at large, I guarantee it won't be long before he'll begin acting like a jerk toward you. Someone who doesn't treat others with kindness and respect is typically someone who has a feeling that he's better than everyone else. Having a superiority complex is a sign of a lack of empathy. You certainly don't want to go through life with someone who lacks empathy! You want someone who can put himself in your place and try to understand what you're going through.

Do You Like Yourself When You and Your Guy Are Together?

All the people in our lives push our buttons in unique ways. When you're with your mom, you might love yourself because she treats you like a rock star. When you're with your boss, you might dislike yourself because he makes you feel like a tongue-tied nervous wreck. How do you feel about yourself when you and your guy are together? Do you love the confident, beautiful, smart, witty, sexy, loving, laid-back goddess you are with him, or do you despise the needy, insecure, nagging, emotional, whiny, uptight creature he turns you into? If it's the latter, then sister, the two of you should not go near an altar!

The best kind of person to marry is a person who brings out the best in you. One of the many reasons I love Tamsen so much is that she truly brings my best self to the surface. When I'm with her, I feel so loved, cared for, and special that the most positive parts of my personality shine through. When you're with someone who treats you with contempt or disrespect or, for whatever reason, makes you feel insecure and unsure of yourself, your true spirit is stifled and replaced by someone else, someone you don't even like. If he brings out the worst in you, then he's not someone with whom you should spend a lifetime.

Is He Selfish?

Do his needs always come first? Does he refuse to ever compromise what he wants in order to make you happy? If a man is selfish, it comes through in big and small ways. Selfishness is a flaw that will seep into every aspect of your relationship, including his dealings with your family and friends, household chores, money, sex, and the time you spend together. For instance, if he has something better going on, don't expect him to go to your grandmother's birthday party with you. If he doesn't care for a good friend of yours, don't expect him to be nice to her. If he is watching a football game, don't expect him to help carry the groceries in from the car. In matters of sex, your pleasure will never be a priority. If you're short on cash, don't ask him to spot you a few bucks. If you'd like to see a movie in which he has no interest, better find someone else to accompany you.

If this sounds like your guy, run for the door! Marriage demands give-and-take. Marrying a man who can take but can't give is a stepping-stone to a lifetime of unhappiness.

MATCHING BAGGAGE

We've explored what your current relationship can predict about your future married life, and you've calculated his "I Do" IQ. The next undertaking is to see if his baggage and your baggage match up. The baggage to which I'm referring is your individual feelings on kids, religion, and money. If you don't put your finger on where each of you stands on these central issues before you tie the knot, you run the risk that any differences you have will slowly unravel your life together.

Kids?

About two years ago Matt and I met with a woman who came to us after she had been married to a very successful man. They both worked in the entertainment industry. Her story goes like this:

Manny and Sarah dated for nearly two years, were engaged for another year, and then got married, only to find out that they held different stances on having children. Manny wanted kids; Sarah did not. Neither had known what the other wanted because they had never discussed it. Sarah was a television reporter trying to move up the corporate ladder. With her demanding job and long commute back and forth to work, she had just enough time at the end of each day to get home and get to sleep, so that she could start all over the next day. Her schedule was full. Moreover, the idea of changing diapers and driving to playdates, not to mention nine months of pregnancy, sounded pretty unappealing to her. Sarah was shocked that having children was so important to Manny.

She wasn't the only clueless one, as it had never occurred to Manny, who was one of five kids, that Sarah would not want children. In fact, he assumed she'd be eager to take a break from work to raise their family. After a year their marriage was history.

Sarah and Manny had never talked about having kids because each had assumed the other held the same opinion on the matter. This folly proved to be their undoing. They violated a fundamental principle: when making plans to spend a lifetime together, *assume nothing*. The fact that you're both in love, you get along, and you have a lot in common doesn't mean you share the same priorities and life goals. The only way to know your guy's position on big issues, such as whether he wants kids, is to discuss them with him. It may not be an easy discussion to have, but it's something you must resolve if you're thinking of planning a life with him. Then, when you do find out his position, don't turn it around to suit your needs. Don't delude yourself that he will change his mind or come around to your way of thinking eventually. If it turns out that you two have opposing stances, it's something you both must be prepared to confront. Don't hang on to hope that time will work out your differences. It won't; it will only emphasize them. If children are important to you, and he doesn't want any, you're going to have to rethink if this is the man for you, and vice versa if he wants them and you don't. Don't wait to figure it out two years into your marriage.

Money Matters

 If your potential husband doesn't subscribe to the motto that a penny saved is a penny earned, and saving money for a rainy day is important to you, don't spend another minute of your time wondering how you will change him. One of the major sources of arguments among couples is money. Therefore, before you even think about saying your "I dos," you must say, "I disclose." It is critical to nail down where both of you stand on situations surrounding your finances. The marriage license doesn't come with a financial spreadsheet that is going to organize all of your

payables and receivables. Money conversations are seldom fun, but it's better to have them now than with a mediator, fighting over "that's mine, this is yours, and the lawyer gets the rest!" Take a look at the list we've put together of money matters that need hashing out:

1. **Nice assets.** You both need to put it all out on the table. He needs to disclose his, and you need to disclose yours.

2. **I owe you.** Is there an outstanding balance that either of you owes? Have you discussed how to deal with debt, budgets, and what would happen if either of you were out of work? The best way to approach this type of discussion is to couch it as a talk about how to go about reaching your future financial goals as a couple. Discussing each other's current debts, current earnings, and future earning potential as a means to reach financial goals is a way to accept where each is currently while at the same time making a plan to get to a better financial place together as a team. You need to sort matters out beforehand, because once you're married, it all goes into and comes out of the same pot.

3. **Who pays?** This is the time to figure out what your paychecks will cover each month, how the bills will be divided, and who will be in charge of sending payments off when due. Sometimes couples work together to get the bills paid, but more often than not, one person has a better head for keeping track

of the bills than the other. If this is the case with you and yours, think about designating that person as the official bill payer. This is a smart way to avoid a situation in which you thought he paid, he thought you paid, and in reality no one paid.

Religion

 More people than I can wave a stick at have come to us saying that religion is not important to them, because they are "spiritual," and that it is OK if they are set up with someone who has different beliefs. While this might work in some instances, many times after people get married and have children, they gravitate toward the religion in which they were raised. If it happens that the husband or wife is of a different faith, a rift could develop in the relationship. That's why I counsel you to give serious thought to what your religious differences might mean as you grow and evolve.

The chief consideration is how your different religious beliefs will impact your children. Can you agree to raise your children under the influence of just one of your religions, or would you rather expose them to both and let them decide which—if either—is a better fit for them when they're older? Also, if you are religious and your dream groom is not, don't assume he will eventually embrace your beliefs. If you do, I confidently predict you'll be disappointed.

••••• WHAT ARE YOUR INTENTIONS? •••••

Having put your guy on the hot seat and checked his baggage against yours, you're back in our spotlight. This section will help you ascertain if you're getting married for the right reasons. It's not meant to put a damper on your wedding party; it's simply meant to give you a chance to check your intentions. Toward that end, cast your eyes on what we've learned over the years after talking to countless happy and unhappy couples about why they decided to get hitched:

The Wrong Reasons to Get Married

❑ **You feel pressure from your family and society.** If your mother is hounding you to find a husband, or if you feel that you are diminished without a man, this is not the right reason to get married. Instead of having a relationship with someone, you may need to spend some time working on your own confidence and sense of self-worth.

❑ **You don't want to be alone.** Of course it's not much fun to go to the movies alone or attend a wedding without a date. Still, there are too many unhappy couples out there who are together simply because they don't want to be alone. It is often better to be lonely alone than lonely with someone.

❑ **You hope to make your relationship stronger.** Buying rings, standing before your friends and family and repeating vows, and then getting a marriage certificate will not make your relationship stronger. A marriage should be icing on the wedding cake. If you are in an unhealthy, insecure, and unhappy relationship, mouthing the phrase "I do" won't fix it.

☐ **You want to get over your ex or your divorce.** I don't care if your ex-husband found a new wife on match.com six months after your divorce. You should not be getting married to show him that you too can be happy without him in your life.

☐ **You fear losing him.** Don't marry someone just to keep him in your life.

☐ **You want financial security.** We often hear people joke about having a "sugar daddy," but marrying simply for money can be very lonely and often results in a marriage with imbalance of power. If financial security is what you want, then sister, work hard to achieve success on your own. It is the twenty-first century, after all!

☐ **You want a wedding.** While the wedding industry makes it exciting to be a bride, your wedding day is only one day in your life. Let me repeat myself: it is one day in your life. When you get married, you are committing to someone for a lifetime! Once the honeymoon's over, it's back to reality, and if the reality is that you're not in love with your husband, you're in big trouble. Think of a wedding as a party to celebrate your goal of sharing a life together, not the goal in and of itself.

⌐ **You worry about your age.** You are never too old to wear white, walk down the aisle, or find your soul mate. Age, therefore, should not be a factor in determining when you get married or, more important, the person you marry.

The Right Reasons to Get Married

⌐ **You are in love with one another.** Love can be difficult for some people to define, but you definitely know it when you are in it. Granted, love alone will not make a relationship work, but it is critical to the foundation of a solid relationship. Love means you know the other person's weaknesses and accept them.

⌐ **The timing is right for both of you.** You must spend enough time getting to know your partner to be sure that you're in a healthy, solid relationship. It is obligatory that you get past the "lust" stage and move into the "trust" stage.

⌐ **You want to share your life with him.** It's a wonderful thing to find someone with whom you want to share your life. We get only one pass on this earth, and if you can find someone to share all of the amazing, magical experiences that life has in store, then I say again: Go for it!

Our own intention is that after reading this chapter, you'll be spurred to spend less time thinking about your engagement ring and wedding day and more time determining if you'll be able to live with the consequences—namely your current boy-friend. Once he has that platinum wedding band on his finger, he's not going to magically transform into the man you want him to be. Not even close. He'll be the man he is right now, only with a new ring on his left hand and the right to half your assets. So, you'd better make sure the man he is now is a man with whom you can spend a lifetime.

TOP TEN REASONS MARRIAGES DON'T WORK

1. Infidelity

2. Sexual incompatibility

3. Money problems

4. Lack of communication

5. One partner outgrows the other

6. Neglect of the relationship due to children, family, career

7. Physical or emotional abuse

8. Religious or cultural differences

9. Drug or alcohol abuse

10. Differences in career and personal goals

WHY I ASKED HER . . .

Of course, I initially had a physical attraction to her, but more important, I caught a glimpse of her inner beauty, huge heart, caring nature, immense generosity, and playful personality. In my eyes, she was the embodiment of the expression of love and virtue, which she shared compassionately with me. It was at that point that I fell in love with her and knew I wanted to spend the rest of my life with her.

—*Dan, married to Pilar for six years*

ON HIS KNEES

During their trip to Jamaica, Jessica and Tom went scuba diving. After they had done a little exploring, their instructor waved them over. They swam toward him, and he pointed to an enormous seashell on the ocean floor. Tom picked up the shell and pulled out a note that was written in waterproof ink. He handed it to Jessica. The note read: "Let's take the plunge: will you marry me?"

Ben and Susan were strolling through Jackson Square in New Orleans when Ben insisted they stop at the easel of a street artist who was drawing caricatures. They sat side by side as the artist drew their picture. When he was finished, he called the couple over to take a look at his masterpiece. When Susan saw Ben's likeness, she began to laugh, but her laughter was cut short when she noticed that cartoon Ben was holding a sign that said, "Will you marry me?"

Colin and Amanda went to see the Celtics play. As usual there was a giveaway during each break. During the last break, the team's mascot, Lucky the Leprechaun, was giving away a basketball signed by the team. Colin and Amanda, both lifetime Celtics fans, screamed enthusiastically for the prize. To Amanda's delight, she won. When the oversize leprechaun held the ball in front of her, instead of the players' names were the words "Will you marry me?"

Each of these proposals is based on a true story. If you'll put the advice we've given you into practice, I foretell that you'll soon be on the receiving end of your own proposal. Once you've got that diamond ring on your finger, you'll want to start planning your trip to the altar (or maybe the justice of the peace). Having done what we could to help you wade through how to snag the proposal, or determine if you even want it, we believe we'd be remiss if we didn't give you the goods on three final slippery situations you'll have to address before you can start your march down the aisle. First, we'll give you the scoop on how you can put your two cents into your engagement ring, and then we'll fill you in on the prenup protocols. Finally, we'll dispense the straight dope on how to best engage in the dreaded (by him, anyway) wedding planning with him.

Before we get to those premarital matters, though, we'd like to touch on one final preproposal point. To wit: should you bring up the subject of marriage?

•••• BURSTING WITH THE QUESTION ••••

As we mentioned in the beginning of the book, the traditional roles of men and women that held steady for centuries have in the past fifty years experienced a massive upheaval. The transition is far from over, and the chips have yet to fall where they will. During this interim, mass confusion abounds. One major area of consternation surrounds the traditional view that it's the man's place to ask the woman to marry him, despite the fact that today, relationships between men and women have moved in the direction of greater equality, and in many cases total equality. This being so, men maintain substantial power in relationships, since they get to decide if and when they will go to the altar. It follows that this state of affairs gives women a sense of powerlessness in their relationships.

A prime example is my friend Felicia. A feminist through and through, Felicia is a strong, independent woman who exudes girl power. She's in charge of a large staff at work, she's the captain of her softball team, she owns her own apartment in the city, and she even has a pilot's license. This woman could single-handedly run the world! Despite all of her strength and assertiveness, she refuses to bring up the topic of marriage with her boyfriend. She just can't force herself to break the social contract that was set down so many millennia before. In every other way her relationship is fifty-fifty.

When I asked Felicia why she wouldn't bring up the topic, the best answer this intelligent, articulate woman could give me was, "I just don't feel that it's my place." With each passing month, I watch Felicia become more and more frustrated with her boyfriend for not proposing. Writing this book has opened my eyes to just how common Felicia's predicament is. This is one unspoken cultural rule that obviously isn't going away anytime soon. So, what's a girl in limbo to do?

You Have Our Blessing

Matt and I believe a good rule of thumb for the period of transition we're in today is that if a woman has been in a long-term relationship with a guy, and she believes it's time for the relationship to be taken to the next level, then yes, it's absolutely OK for her to raise the topic of marriage. Take note that bringing up the topic of marriage is not the same as formally proposing. I'm not telling you to drop down on one knee and ask him to marry you. I'm saying it's right as rain for you to initiate the marriage conversation in order to gauge his position and to make yours clear.

Forget all that nonsense you've heard over the years about not bringing up marriage for fear of scaring him away. That bromide has merit if you're just starting to date a guy, but if you've been in a long-term relationship with a man, and you're starting to feel as if you're in limbo, you have every right to discuss the future of your partnership. Sure, some men man-

WHY I ASKED HER . . .

I want to say that I asked her for all of the sappy reasons you are supposed to give, but I guess the truth of the matter is that I simply loved her. Karen was fun to be with and didn't really demand a lot from me. I think that is what really attracted me to her, since my career was taking off at the time. She was all the things that you think of when you think of love. She was patient, kind, and forgiving, and she still is today. Plus, she is a wonderful mother to our two daughters.

—*Booker, married to Karen for fifteen years*

age to pull off the proposal. They buy the ring, they get down on one knee—the whole shebang. Notwithstanding, most guys these days need a little push in the right direction, for all of the reasons we've paraded before you in the previous pages.

Truth or Consequences

A good way to think about it is to consider the consequences of *not* bringing it up. Either you live the rest of your born days in limbo, or you dump him without telling him why. Dumb and dumber! Given the options available, the best course of action by far is to take the initiative and broach the topic on your end. However, before you do, be sure you've adopted all of the advice in this book that pertains to your particular situation, put it into practice, and given it enough time to take hold. Don't skip this step, because the rules of conduct contained between the covers of this book will either (1) save you the trouble of having to open the marriage discussion in the first place, because he'll have beaten you to the punch, or (2) make him much more willing to embrace the idea of marrying sexy, independent, fabulous, financially sound, fit, adventurous you.

Now that you know our current position on whether you should bring up the topic of marriage (I'm sure further down the road we'll have to reassess—hopefully, by 2050, we'll be working on our book *Why Hasn't She Proposed?*), here are a few pointers on having the marriage discussion:

  Timing, timing, timing. Be sure you bring up the topic at an opportune time—when you are in a good place, he is in a good place, and your relationship is in a good place. You don't want to approach him with the idea of spending the rest of his life with you right after you've lost your job or gotten into a raucous fight with your family. To prime the pump, for a few weeks or months beforehand, work on giving yourself a mini-makeover, so that you're looking especially hot. Work out, do something fabulous with your hair, try some new makeup and fashion strategies—you know the drill.

Similarly, make sure he's bright-eyed and bushy-tailed. Don't hit him with the marriage convo right after he's found out that his rent is going up 50 percent or that he's been passed over for a promotion. Also, your relationship has to be in one of its good patches. Specifically, I recommend bringing up the topic on a night when the two of you have been having a great time together. However, let it come up organically. Don't plan a big dinner and make it appear that you've orchestrated the evening specifically for a talk about marriage. In fact, don't pick a specific night to do the deed. Instead, start working on your minimakeover, pick a window of time during which to act—say, sometime in June—and then just wait for one of those nights when you're having a blast to start the discussion.

Keep it positive. I can't coach you on exactly what to say, because you know your guy, and by now you know the best way to get through to him. I do suggest easing into the conversation. Perhaps say something such as, "Do you think about our future together?" Then take it from there. Strive to be open, honest, and straightforward about what you want and where you stand. Don't play word games with him or leave anything unsaid in the hopes that he can "figure out" how you feel by your tone of voice or expression. As has been established, that's not how men communicate. The overriding guideline here is to keep the conversation positive. Kicking, screaming, and crying will get you nowhere in this delicate tête-à-tête.

Don't pin him down . . . yet. Don't expect a "yes" or "no" during the initial foray. Maybe he's already thought about it and has an answer ready for you, but this could also be the first time he's entertaining the idea. In the latter case, it's only fair that you give him some time to digest it—but not too much time. Pondering his feelings and stalling are two different things, and this intrigue needs to reach conclusion sooner rather than later. He owes you an answer.

 **Brace yourself.** Be prepared for whatever his answer might be. If his answer is yes, he does want to eventually marry you, then you must get a sense of whether your timetables mesh. Beyond that aspect, try to avoid getting carried away by details. You don't want to take the entire element of surprise out of your impending proposal. You must also be prepared if his answer is the dreaded no, he does not see marriage in the future for the two of you. Before you give voice to the topic, you must consider how a negative response will impact your relationship. If you should decide beforehand that you couldn't stay with him if he didn't want to marry you, then you must be prepared to walk away. If you currently live with him, this means wrangling with the logistics of moving out if you decide a relationship that will not lead to marriage is not for you.

••••• HOW TO BE THE RING LEADER •••••

Did you see the episode of "Sex and the City" in which Carrie finds the engagement ring that Aidan picked out before he proposed . . . and she hates it? It is a scene that still sends chills through me. No woman wants to be in that position! Obviously, no man wants to be put in that position either. Without question, he wants you to love the ring every bit as much as you want to love it. Since you're going to be wearing the ring for the rest of your life (or at least until you get a bigger stone for your tenth anniversary!), it stands to reason that you'd want to make sure it's the perfect one for you. These days, many men do ask for their girlfriend's input on the ring. Oftentimes, couples shop for the ring together; then he tucks it away until he can "surprise" her with it when he proposes. However, other guys still want to include that element of surprise in the proposal.

If your guy is one of those brave souls who choose to go it alone, there are a few things you can do to assure that you have a say in the ring, albeit behind the scenes. For starters, make sure your fiancé-to-be knows your style. You can convey your taste to him more subtly through your jewelry. If you're wearing a necklace, ring, bracelet, or pair of ear-

FROM C TO SHINING C

If you're going with your guy to shop for the ring, here's what you need to know:

- The *cut* of a diamond affects how light passes through it. "Round brilliant" is the most common cut. The *shape* of a diamond is its physical shape. The most popular shapes are round and oval, with other common shapes being emerald and princess.

- *Clarity* refers to how easy it is to see the imperfections of a diamond.

- Diamonds range in *color* from clear to a faint yellow. The color classifications of clear diamonds range from D to Z. D applies to the most transparent, clear, colorless diamonds, while Z is light yellow.

- The *carat* of a diamond refers to its weight. The heavier and larger a diamond, the more it costs.

- Among the four Cs—cut, clarity, color, and carat—it is the cut that matters most, because it is what gives the stone its sparkle and shine.

- Don't buy a diamond that doesn't come with a *cert*, a document that lists its clarity, color, cut, and carat count. The four independent labs that make these determinations are the GIA, IGI, EGL, and AGS.

- Clarity, color, and cut are more important to the value of a diamond than size.

☐ Platinum is thirty-five times rarer than gold, so it stands to reason that platinum settings are more expensive than gold. Despite the price, most people prefer platinum to gold, because it is more durable and also because it provides a cleaner background for the clear color of diamonds.

☐ According to the jewelry industry, a man should spend two times the salary he earns in one month on an engagement ring. According to this book, a man should spend what he can afford on an engagement ring!

rings with a stone that's in the shape you prefer, point it out to him. Maybe even go so far as to say, "Check out my new earrings. I had to choose between these round-shaped diamonds or square-shaped. I thought the round-shaped were so much prettier!" Second, find ways to impress upon him that when it comes to expensive jewelry, you're a platinum girl—unless, of course, you're a gold girl. While you're at it, tell your sister, mother, and best friends exactly the kind of engagement ring you want. If you are close to his mother and sisters, tell them as well. If he's like most men we know, he will consult with them in choosing the ring. To add to his knowledge base, give him a hand, so to speak: leave a ring that fits on your ring finger around the house, so he can use it to know your size.

● ● ● ● ● WHAT'S UP WITH THE PRENUP? ● ● ● ● ●

Prenup. Yuck! Just those six letters conjure up visions of a nasty divorce, ugly words, and, of course, an end to the proposal you worked so hard to get. As onerous as they may seem, prenups are a reality in a society in which nearly half of all marriages end in divorce. It's not as romantic as thinking about diamonds and dresses and flowers, but a prenup is definitely something on which you should at least educate yourself.

In brief, a prenuptial agreement is a contract between two people who are about to get married. It dictates how assets will be distributed in the event of divorce or death. Many people erroneously think prenups are aimed toward cheating one partner out of the other's assets down the line. While the contract states the amount that each party will receive in the event of a divorce, specific terms of prenups vary widely from couple to couple.

Here's one reason to think about having a prenup that may not have occurred to you: because folks are waiting longer to get married, when they do tie the knot, they have more stuff, which often means they have more debt. I have a friend who had accumulated significant debt getting her doctorate. Her fiancé, on the other hand, had avoided any debt. My friend didn't like to think that one day her soon-to-be husband could be saddled with her obligations, so for her, it wasn't about protecting her assets; it was about shielding her betrothed from her creditors.

That's not to say that a prenup designed to lay out the asset division in the case of a divorce isn't also worth considering. Many women believe that if he asks you to sign a prenup, that means he doesn't love you. This presumption is also erroneous. Many men and women have gone through a divorce before— that of their parents. Some decided back then that if they ever were to marry, it would only be with a prenup. So, being asked to sign off on a prenup might have nothing to do with you and everything to do with his experience with his parents' divorce. Also, you should know that men's magazines often have articles about how to get a woman to sign a prenup. All told, it most likely is a matter your guy has thought about way before he met you.

 WHY I ASKED HER . . .

After a few years of dating, it became obvious that the relationship was one that I thoroughly enjoyed and with which I was comfortable. We had a lot in common, we were friends (very important in a marriage), and our differences were complementary and compatible. It became obvious to me that this was the right time to make it an exclusive and long-term relationship. I proposed on New Year's Eve.

—Kal, married to Janet for forty years

At a minimum, invest some time becoming informed about what a prenup is all about and how it might benefit your situation. If you decide it is something to consider, don't be afraid to talk openly about it with your guy. In that same spirit, if he approaches you about it, be open to listening to his reasoning without jumping to the conclusion that he doesn't have faith in your upcoming nuptials.

A GUY'S GUIDE TO WEDDING PLANNING

Chew on this morsel, ladies: wedding planning is more stressful to a guy than proposing. He's seen it in the movies, he's read about the horrors in books, and he's even heard about it firsthand if he was ever a groomsman sometime during the course of his singlehood. Listen, as in tune as Matt is with dating, love, women, image, and all the rest, he was in no way eager or able to make decisions regarding our wedding. Here's my opinion on how much or little to include your counterpart in the planning:

☐ **The dress.** Obviously, he will have no involvement with this. You'll do well to leave him out of it. That includes not leaving wedding porn all over the house. If you have subscribed to a billion wedding magazines, stash them (and all of your adhesive notes) in one location. It's not necessary for him to see that you have narrowed it down to 211 dresses and that you are still on the hunt for the perfect one.

☑ **The venue.** This is one area in which I believe he should have a say, but only if he wants to. Matt was willing to go to a number of locations with me to look at the venues. I scheduled them all over two days, and by the end of the second day, we had selected Tavern on the Green in Central Park. I didn't make a big deal out of it and didn't spread it out for months. Follow my lead and keep it simple if you can. If you do want to see multiple places, go scope them out yourself first, and then take him only to your top five favorite ones.

☑ **The food and cake.** The way it typically unfolds is that neither one of you will actually even have a chance to eat, since you will be running to take pictures, talk to family and friends, and then leave for your wedding night! Since his personal tastes—vegetarian versus meat and potatoes—are not paramount, my advice: don't eat breakfast; then grab a friend (or two) and handle the tasting yourself. The upside of your carrying this burden is that you will bond with your girlfriend while not bothering him. Plus, you get a free meal!

☑ **The registry.** I don't care how dearly you want him to help you select the perfect blender, leave him out of this unless he is dying to take a trip to Bed Bath & Beyond. Enlist your mom, sister, best girlfriend, or best gay friend for this jaunt. Or, you can do it all these days from the comfort of your own living room. Registering online is easier than ever!

☑ **The honeymoon.** Couples tend to plan the honeymoon together. To him even more so than to you, this is a fun, relaxing trip after all the stress, so give him the chance to have his input. That way you can tailor the trip to both of your likings.

⊐ **The photographer, the music, the toasts.** It goes without saying that he doesn't care about the photographer, the music, or the toasts. While it would be nice to have his input on the toasts, it's really not necessary. Make sure you handle this as well.

⊐ **The invitations.** I took Matt to the stationer after I had selected the invitations we would use. He simply said yes when I asked him if he liked them. If I showed him three invitations today, I am not convinced he could pick out which one we sent.

⊐ **The guest list.** Ask him to give you the names of his friends and family he would like to invite, and then ask his mother or sister to help you with the rest. While it may not seem fair that you are doing so much of the heavy lifting, it did take plenty of courage for him to lift his credit card out of his wallet and buy the ring.

HAPPILY EVER AFTER: MAKING LOVE LAST

 While I don't "propose" to know everything, I do know one thing: you must put your relationship first. If you have both decided that you want to spend your lives together, then work and people, even meddling

family members, should never come between the two of you. I have learned through my experiences that things work best in my life when my relationship comes first. This is certainly not to say that I revolve every decision of my waking day around when we are going to dinner, to the movies, or to a tropical getaway, but I do make sure that I don't take out my stresses from work on Tamsen and that we keep the lines of communication open so that there is no room for "misunderstandings" regarding our lives, feelings, and what we both want for the future.

Here we offer you some of the simple rules by which we try to live:

Share the first kiss . . . yet again. You remember it. It made your toes tingle. Don't let that feeling ever go away. No matter how tired I am, I make sure that I kiss Tamsen before she walks out the door each morning, and she treats me the same way.

Let your fingers do the talking. Send him a text every now and then. Let him know you are thinking about him. It can be funny, sexy, or cute, but there's nothing like a woman who can make a man smile in the middle of a stressful day.

Make a date. Being engaged or married doesn't mean you can't date like teenagers. Tamsen and I love to go out on the weekends, plan a Saturday at the movies, or just pretend we are kids again and run around at the beach. Make an effort not to lose the spark, as can easily happen when real life tries to take over.

⌐ **Run away.** No, not on your wedding day, but afterward. Take a last-minute, unplanned trip to nowhere. Don't tell anyone where you are going, put that BlackBerry on mute, and enjoy yourselves . . . alone.

⌐ **Shape up.** The honeymoon will be glorious, but don't let yourself go when you're back at the grind just because you won the man over. Keep in shape together for your mind, health, and body. Beyond those benefits, it's a turn-on to sweat together!

⌐ **Don't get personal.** Watch what you say. You can't take back hurtful words that cut to the core. If you don't have something civil or at least noncombative to say, don't say anything at all. Words can do more damage than you know, so don't be personal just to strike out during an argument.

⌐ **Pay attention to the little things.** Once upon a time, you used to buy him mushy cards or show up with just your coat on and nothing under it. Don't lose the desire that drew you to each other in the first place. There are few things more attractive to a man than being in lust with the woman he loves.

Now, dear reader, it's nearly time to put this book away. (We do mean "away"; this is not a book to leave out on your shelf. Hide it or, better yet, give it to another gal who's waiting around for her guy to pop the question.) You need to get on with putting the advice that fits your situation to work. To fill us in on how everything goes, or if you have any questions that you think we could help you with, visit our site at whyhasnthe.com. We hope to hear from you, and we can't wait to get an invite to the big day!

SIGNS HE'S ABOUT TO POP THE QUESTION

1. He starts window-shopping. When a man takes to pausing in front of windows to some of your favorite jewelry shops, you can pretty much assume that you have a ringer!

2. He starts saving. This is a harbinger that your man is ready to tie the knot or at least tie up the loose ends on his financial situation. If you observe that he is making fewer trips to Starbucks and doesn't buy the latest version of the iPhone, he may be saving up for another type of "ring."

3. The word _we_ suddenly appears. A vast majority of the guys we know have a tendency to forget that this word exists in the English language until they are ready to start thinking about sharing their lives with another person. If the love of your life is starting to use the words _we_ and _us_, it is suggestive that he is looking to make the pairing permanent.

4. He becomes kid friendly. Prior to this stage, he may have avoided children altogether, but suddenly your man is holding babies like a politician, is making goo-goo sounds when he's in line at the grocery store and sees a kid in the cart in front of him, and is glad to have your nephew tag along on Sundays. He may not be quite ready to be a proud papa, but he is definitely laying the groundwork for a future together.

5. **He is a little apprehensive and nervous.** Don't be alarmed. This does not mean that he is getting cold feet. It can be scary to drop down on one knee, just after having had to approach your dad for permission! Imagine the pressure! Give him a little space. If he is planning a proposal, it's probable that he is trying to make sure it's perfect and is a little nervous about its going just the way he wants it to.

6. **He goes willingly to weddings.** It wasn't so long ago that you had to make "deals" to get him to darken the doorway of your friends' weddings. For instance, you agreed to let him watch football for three consecutive days in exchange for his accompanying you to your best friend's nuptials. Suddenly that has all dissolved, and he is more than willing to go see your BFF get hitched. If that weren't miracle enough, once you are there, oh my goodness, he is actually paying attention to the number of groomsmen and the style of tuxedo they are all wearing. Do not ruin the experience by showing surprise. Act as if he is being perfectly normal, and restrain yourself from scoffing at anything or acting negative about the wedding. If he is interested in your friend's wedding, he is mentally preparing for his own!

7. **He and you take a sudden trip to see your parents.** This
is one time you don't ask any questions. Your boyfriend
may be getting up the nerve to ask your dad for your hand
in marriage if he is the traditional type. We have heard
of plenty of brides-to-be who made joint visits to their
parents several times before the guy actually proposed
(because it took him a few runs to work up the courage to
actually approach the dad). Do your part to bring the mission off without an abort. For instance, give him time alone
with your father, and don't cling to him or ask him what he
is doing every second.

APPENDIX

POPPING THE QUESTION

THEN AND NOW

 "Will you marry me?" Four little words that women long to hear. Magical though they may be, those four little words are only one part of the time-honored ritual we refer to as a "marriage proposal." In addition to the question itself, there is the getting down on one knee and the presentation of the ring, and, of course, prior to that whole scene the guy has to formally ask the woman's father for "her hand." Sounds like a lot of brouhaha, doesn't it? If only it were that simple!

Men, being a competitive bunch, have transformed that rite of passage into a full-on competition. No longer can you just take a woman to a nice restaurant and get down on bended knee between the entree and the dessert. Oh no! You have to hire an airplane to skywrite the question in the wild blue yonder or drop a pile of cash to have a stadium flash it up on a gigantic screen during a major sports event. It makes you long for simpler times—back when a man could just bop his woman of choice over the head with a club and drag her back to his cave. (Kidding; no angry e-mails, please!)

The pressure for a man to make the event the most romantic proposal ever has reached the same level as the pressure to throw the most special, most memorable wedding bash in the history of humankind. Technically speaking, we guys don't get to "pop" the question. The verb *pop* suggests that one day we come up with the fantastic idea of marrying the woman we love, and we just pass it by her casually over our morning cup of coffee. "Mornin', hon. How did you sleep? Oh say, how 'bout we get hitched?" No, there's no popping. It's more like launching a theatrical production. And you ladies wonder why we guys aren't dropping like flies down on bended knee!

Since our book focuses on such a strange, pressure-laden set of circumstances, Tamsen and I thought we would be negligent if we didn't delve a little into how the heck the current proposal protocol came to be. We also thought it would be fun to take a gander at the creative, tacky, wacky, off-the-charts ways some hopeful husbands are approaching it. Let's start by taking a peek into the past to see how this getting-down-on-bended-knee thing came to be.

••••• PROPOSING BACK IN THE DAY •••••

Why get married? The instant response to this question is almost always, "Because of love." Not so fast there. Marrying for love, alack, is a completely modern notion. In Western civilization, until fairly recently, a marriage proposal was nothing more than a business proposition. Money and power decided who married whom. Love did not enter the picture. If the couple comprised a couple of peasants, then Mom and Pop did the matchmaking. There was no getting down on bended knee. The "proposal" went more like this: "I'll give you my daughter to be your wife (servant), plus a cow and two pigs."

If the couple were of noble blood, marriage was more about matters of state. Matches were made to form alliances, join properties, and settle disagreements. For those chosen few, the proposal went more like this: "Our nation giveth you the king's daughter as a token of our agreement to stop beating the crap out of ye on the battlefield. Oh, and we also promise to have your back if any of your enemies attack you." Once the paperwork was signed, sealed, and delivered, there was some type of ceremony, and that was that.

An Innocent Plea

The history books say that it wasn't until 1215 that the notion of setting a specific lapse of time between the marriage arrangement and the marriage ceremony came about. The idea of a formal "engagement" period was the brainchild of Pope Innocent III. Silver or iron rings were to be worn during the period of engagement to seal the deal. The rings were placed on the fourth finger of the left hand because that is where the "vena amoris," or vein of love, runs straight to the heart. Moving on, we guys have Archduke Maximillian of Austria to thank for the upgrade of the simple silver or iron ring to a diamond ring. In 1477, his royal archdukeness gave his betrothed, Mary of Burgundy, the first recorded diamond engagement ring. According to lore, the ring was set with thin, flat pieces of diamonds in the shape of an *M*.

Courting Favor

It's not exactly clear how the act of getting down on one knee originated. Historians believe that it goes back to medieval times when a knight would kneel at the beginning of a joust in the hopes that his ladylove would toss him a flower to show him that she fancied him too. As for the custom that calls for the hopeful husband-to-be to ask his girlfriend's father if he can have her "hand in marriage," that's a tradition that harks way back to the good old Roman days and a custom called the "joining of hands." The prospective groom would give the bride-to-be's father a coin, and her hand would be passed from her father's clasp to the warm palm of her betrothed.

While many guys continue this man-to-man tradition, some say they believe this step is too antiquated to carry out. Although most grooms-to-be view it as a way to show the bride-to-be's father respect, some see it as disrespectful of the future fiancée. They say it discounts the fact that she is an independent, adult woman. It sort of makes it seem that she is a family possession. Personally, I had no problem asking Tamsen's dad for her lovely hand. For the record, Tamsen didn't have a problem with it either. We both felt it was a good way to show her father that we loved and respected him, in addition to making him feel included in our decision to get married.

TAKING A LEAP: SHE PROPOSES TO HIM

Another proposal custom that goes back several centuries gives women the right to propose to the man of their choice on February 29, which comes around only in leap years. Way back when, the leap year day was not recognized in English law. Since the day itself had no legal status, all traditions also had no status during those twenty-four hours. Thus, if a woman was tired of waiting for a guy to get to it and pop the ques-

WEDDING CUSTOMS UNVEILED

☐ **Bridal bouquet.** The tradition of the bridal bouquet dates back to Roman times. The bride would hold a bunch of potent herbs that were meant to keep evil spirits at bay. Eventually, the tradition of holding herbs gave way to the more attractive option of holding a bouquet of fragrant flowers.

☐ **White wedding dress.** The custom for brides to wear white for their weddings began in the Victorian era. A bride of that period was expected to be a pure, chaste virgin. Get it? White equals pure. We bow to the fabulous Empress Eugénie, the bride of Napoleon III, for the elaborateness of the modern white wedding gowns with which we're familiar today.

☐ **Best man.** The German Goths were responsible for the tradition of the best man. Often the Goths had to sweep their brides off their feet, literally. When the supply of available women ran low in a community, men had to kidnap women from neighboring communities. Nabbing a bride-to-be was totally a two-man job, so a guy had no choice but to take along his closest, most trustworthy buddy to assist him in the caper. The best man also literally had to have the groom's back during the marriage ceremony just in case the bride's family showed up uninvited to reclaim her.

⌐ **Honeymoon.** The honeymoon is one of the more ancient of all wedding traditions, dating back four thousand years to the Babylonian period. Back in Babylonia, the father of the bride would give the groom the wedding gift of all the honey beer or honey wine that he could drink. The Babylonian calendar was based on the phases of the moon, and it took the groom about one month to consume all of the honey beer or wine. Owing to this policy, the period after the wedding came to be known as the "honeymonth," which ultimately came to be called the "honeymoon."

⌐ **Bridesmaids.** Roman law called for ten witnesses to be present at all weddings. The bridesmaids were required to wear dresses similar to the bride's, and the groomsmen were required to wear clothes similar to the groom's. This was done in an attempt to fool evil spirits who were looking to cause mischief for the couple. No one is quite sure about the impetus of the modern tradition of dressing bridesmaids in hideous gowns that they won't ever wear again despite the bride's assurance that they can "just shorten it."

⌐ **Wedding veil.** In ancient times, grooms not only didn't choose their own brides but also often didn't even get to meet her before the wedding. To prevent the groom from running for the door upon catching his first glimpse of the bride, she hid her face with a veil.

tion, she could take matters into her own hands and ask him to marry her. According to some accounts, any man who turned down the proposition had to pay a fine. The fine ranged from a kiss to a payment for a silk dress to a pair of new gloves.

This tradition is still given credence. On the most recent leap year day, which was in 2008, newspapers galore ran light-hearted articles about the old custom, and some included tips for how a woman wishing to act on it should go about proposing. In one article, women were advised not to get down on one knee, especially if they were in stilettos. Lake Vyrnwy Hotel, in Wales, even offered a "leap year proposal package" at a cost of $348 per person. The package consisted of two nights at the four-star hotel, a full Welsh breakfast, and dinner for two at the hotel's Tower restaurant. In addition, if the guy said yes, the hotel gave the couple a complimentary bottle of champagne with which to celebrate. And if the schmuck said no, the "burly hotel staff" promised to "escort him from the premises and present the woman with a cuddly Welsh dragon, a box of tissues, and some chocolates to comfort her." She was also given "the bottle of bubbly so that she could drink a toast to her lucky escape." The bad news is that leap year only comes every four years. In the meantime, who knows, maybe you'll decide to take the leap, leap year or no leap year. The precedent has been set most fashionably: both Charlotte and Miranda proposed to their guys on "Sex and the City"!

THE WOW FACTOR

 Even though the basics of the ritual hail from the past, the modern wedding proposal is distinctly a product of our times. It has followed the current trend of its own aftermath—the wedding. Weddings are now lavish affairs at which anything goes. Couples feel and, unfortunately, give into an underlying pressure to make their weddings bigger, better, more "personalized," and more expensive than the next couple's. As part of the spillover, guys are feeling this same pressure in the realm of popping the question. Innumerable articles appear in magazines and online with instructions and advice for men on the topic. One article lists the biggest mistakes a guy can make in performing this task, such as proposing empty-handed or in front of a crowd.

Businesses have even cropped up to help men "produce" their marriage proposals. One such company is Your Hand in Marriage. On its website, the company states that it is "solely focused on igniting the thought process of the soon-to-be groom." Company representatives offer to be physically present during the proposal, but "behind the scenes," to make sure everything goes off without a slip. The consultants answer questions such as the following:

- How to get the proposal written in the sky
- How to get the proposal announced at a special show or event
- How to get the proposal on television

So much for taking her to your favorite restaurant, getting down on one knee, and asking her to marry you while offering up an outrageously expensive diamond ring. Diamond ring! Big deal! These are the days of fireworks, skywriting, and clever ruses, and if you can throw a cuddly animal into the mix, so much the better.

Personally, I believe all the pressure that's been heaped on the marriage proposal ritual is ridiculous. Let me qualify that: I genuinely appreciate fun and creative marriage proposals. It's the *pressure* to include the wow factor that I deplore. I believe the proposal should be a reflection of both the man's personality and the relationship. A marriage proposal is one occasion in which what matters is what he's saying, not how he's saying it. Having said all that, I enjoy a creative-marriage-proposal story just as much as the next guy. I especially love the weird, wild, and wacky proposals. And who can resist the dish on how celebs popped the question? In that spirit, we conclude by sharing the following tales of cool, weird, wild, and wacky wedding proposals. Although some of the names have been changed, each of these stories is based on an actual incident. Enjoy!

First Search-Engine Wedding Proposal

Moe took his girlfriend, Farah, in to work with him one day, and while they were clowning around on the computer, he suggested they do a search on their own names. After he had typed his name into the Ask Jeeves search engine, it was Farah's turn. Stealthily, Moe knelt down beside her, with the engagement ring he had bought for her at the ready. When Farah typed in her name, up came a picture of her and Moe, along with a link to their under-construction website. The middle portion of the page read in a bright, bold font: "Farah, Will You Marry Me?—Love Moe."

Over the Bridge

When they had just begun dating, Hector and Justine took a walk through a park. They came across a lovely, old wooden bridge. Justine couldn't walk across the uneven beams, because she was wearing high heels. Taking the opportunity to play superhero, Hector swept Justine off her feet and carried her across the bridge. A year or so later, he commissioned a local artist to paint a picture of that same bridge. Hector then presented the picture to Justine. Under the gorgeous likeness were the words, "Justine, let's cross all bridges together from now on. Will you marry me?"

Marry Christmas

Lyle and Kim were high school sweethearts. Everyone expected that they would someday marry. Christmas was Kim's favorite time of year, and moving to New York City with all its festive Christmas decorations had intensified her fondness for the holiday. Since the couple had moved to New York, both of their families had come to spend the holidays with them.

It was their second year in the city, and because Lyle was still in grad school, and they had decided to wait to get engaged until he finished his degree, the furthest thing from Kim's mind was a possible proposal. A few days before Christmas, the couple took their families to Rockefeller Center to go ice-skating. Kim was having a merry time skating with her niece and nephew, but when Lyle swooped in and took her hand, she was thrilled to slow down and skate with just him. When they reached the center of the rink, Lyle abruptly stopped and faced her. "Kim," he said, "I love you more than anything in the world." Then, right there in the middle of the ice, he got down on one knee, held up a ring, and said, "Will you marry me?" With tears in her eyes, Kim said yes. After Lyle placed the beautiful ring on Kim's finger, the crowded rink burst into applause. Kim looked up and saw their family members clapping madly from above. With Kim surrounded by loved ones, during her favorite time of year, Lyle's timing was impeccable.

Silicon Valley Geek Proposes

For a self-proclaimed computer geek, the best way to deliver a marriage proposal is via dependable software. Ergo, that's exactly how a Google software engineer sent his proposal to his girlfriend. The software program in question—Street View, Google Maps' online gallery of street-level paKimmas—captures images by roving vehicle-mounted cameras. The hopeful groom-to-be got the idea when his company announced a planned drive-by of its Mountain View headquarters. As the camera rolled, he held up a sign that read: "Marry me, Suzie!!" Once the images were on the Web, he launched a website and posted his girlfriend's e-mail address on it. When she checked her e-mail in-box, it was full of messages telling her to marry him. How could she refuse?

Home Run

Ike scored a home run when he asked Ida to marry him. Here's how his winning proposal pitch went down: The couple are devoted fans of the Lacrosse Loggers baseball team. On fan appreciation night, Ike managed to arrange for Ida to throw out the first pitch. When the time came, he slipped away to put on a Loggers uniform and catching gear as prearranged and trotted out to the catcher's box to retrieve Ida's practice pitches. With his mask still on, he then walked out to the mound to hand the ball back to her, at which point he removed the catcher's mask to reveal himself. In front of all the fans, he then asked her to marry him.

FURTHER READING

Toxic In-Laws: Loving Strategies for Protecting Your Marriage by Susan Forward

Susan Forward's practical and powerful book speaks to couples coping with what some have described as "toxic" in-laws. The author relays stories from real people who are struggling to free themselves from these relationships. She shows readers what to say, what to do, and how to set limits in their interfamily relationships. If you are up in arms with a set of in-laws who seem like outlaws, this is the book to read.

How to Deal with Your Mother-in-Law (Sisters and Family Included) by Dr. Bree Allinson

Mothers-in-law can be a particular challenge to couples, especially when they are overbearing and controlling. Without intimidating readers, the author points out common issues that couples face on this subject and offers help for those who are constantly at odds with their in-laws.

Why We Love: The Nature and Chemistry of Romantic Love by **Helen Fisher**

> This fascinating book by Helen Fisher offers new insight into the universal phenomenon of romantic love. Fisher worked with a team of scientists to scan the brains of people who had just fallen in love to show what happens when you feel that romantic passion. She reveals what you experience, why you choose one person instead of another, and how romantic love affects your feelings of attachment.

I Promise You: Preparing for a Marriage That Will Last a Lifetime by **Willard Harley Jr.**

> Before you exchange those beautiful shiny rings, you are going to be asked to repeat some heavy promises to one another. Considering the frightening divorce statistics, it is an asset to create a healthy and vibrant marriage in advance of the ceremony itself. Willard Harley offers tips on the ways to do that, along with practical exercises that will help couples evaluate and improve their relationships.

If Love Could Think: Using Your Mind to Guide Your Heart by **Alon Gratch**

> Turn to this text for answers to the age-old questions that apply to any stage of your relationship: why love goes wrong and what to do to make it right. It identifies seven common patterns of failed love and illustrates how all of

these patterns stem from one problem: ambivalence. *If Love Could Think* shows how to break these patterns of failed relationships and find true love.

The Seven Principles for Making a Marriage Work: A Practical Guide by John M. Gottman

Here John Gottman provides seven principles that help guide couples along the path toward a harmonious and long-lasting relationship. *The Seven Principles for Making a Marriage Work* includes questionnaires and exercises to help couples who want their relationships to reach their highest potential.

Why Marriages Succeed or Fail and How You Can Make Yours Last by John M. Gottman

With this entry, John Gottman guides couples through a series of self-tests to show you what kind of marriage you have, your strengths and weaknesses, and what you can do to help your marriage. You will learn how sex affects marriage, why frequent arguing doesn't lead to divorce, and how to recognize attitudes that can doom a marriage.

If Men Could Talk: Unlocking the Secret Language of Men by Alon Gratch

When men do speak, they often use a language that sounds foreign to women. *If Men Could Talk* helps decode why men think and act as they do. The book reveals the male psychology and breaks it down into seven factors. It then provides tools to help you better understand their world.

Women and Money: Owning the Power to Control Your Destiny by Suze Ormond

If you are looking for solid financial advice, Suze Ormond is the person to consult. With a straightforward approach and a supportive tone, she orients readers to the basics of finances. Ormond explores the issues of women and their relationships with money and shares her story of her own evolving relationship with her finances. Learn how best to establish checking and savings accounts, fix your credit rating, save for retirement, set up a will, and purchase home insurance.

The Ultimate Guide to Adult Videos: How to Watch Adult Videos and Make Your Sex Life Sizzle by Violet Blue

Here you have at your fingertips friendly advice on bringing excitement into your sex life. With her wit, expertise, and enthusiasm, sex specialist Violet Blue doles out helpful information for couples, including how to introduce adult films into your relationship.

Men, Love, and Sex: The Complete User's Guide for Women by David Zincsenko and Ted Spiker

> Men confess what turns them on and what turns them off, and readers learn how to turn "for now" into "forever." The authors explain how men act and think and what they are looking for in their relationships.

Passionate Marriage: Keeping Love and Intimacy Alive in Committed Relationships by David Schnarch

> This book sets forth groundbreaking ways of understanding your situation as a couple and tells you how to create new ways to enhance your relationship. *Passionate Marriage* features actions you can take to institute positive changes in your marriage.

RESOURCES

You finally got the ring. Now you need to make an oath to take care of yourself as you enter into what is often the most exciting but stressful time of your life. We are not going to give you a wedding planner, but we do have for you some favorite products and places as a guide to fun and beauty (both inside and outside).

BEAUTY

Makeup

Laurageller.com. When you're in a quandary over makeup, Laura Geller is your girlfriend who knows all. Her products are all baked in Italy. They are not only cool to look at but also luxurious to use, from the Spackle to her famous Brow Tint and Tamer for beautifully shaped brows. If you are feeling a little stressed about everything, you can try some caulk concealer; it's just what every girl needs to get rid of blemishes for good.

Beautyaddicts.com. OK, we are officially addicted to Beauty Addicts. The company's motto is "beauty made simple," and that is exactly what it is. In the product palette, shades and textures complement each other with both edge and timeless style. You can also choose from a system of colors that are designed around the moods and attitudes of today's woman—including flirtatious, casual, professional, and downright glamorous.

Hair

Tedgibsonbeauty.com. No matter how stressed out you may be, you must make sure your tresses don't start feeling the same way. Celebrity stylist Ted Gibson has an amazing line (and we mean amazing) that will nourish your hair, helping it stay healthy, shiny, and glorious from the first date to the wedding date and beyond.

Skin

Nicholasperricone.com. Good skin is always in at Nicholas Perricone. His rejuvenating program of diet, exercise, and skin care can make you look younger and wrinkle free. From Age Prevent to Skin Clear, these products can take your complexion from dull to delicious in no time. Healthy-looking skin is always important, especially when you want to glow on your big day.

FASHION

Clothes

❑ **Topbutton.com** and **Thetopsecret.com.** Topbutton.com is brimming with fabulous fashion and beauty advice and money-saving deals. It gives you the inside scoop on all the leading designer clothing and sample sales in the New York and L.A. metro areas. If you must have it right away, check out the company's sister site, thetopsecret.com. Here members have access to exclusive offers from premier brands with discounts of up to 75 percent off retail. Thetopsecret.com is an invitation-only site, but not to worry: just type in the word *proposed* on the invitation to gain immediate access to major designer discounts!

Bags

❑ **Bagtrends.com.** Wanna know what's going to be hot tomorrow, today? Then get yourself to bagtrends.com, where you will learn how to use your accessories to take any outfit from special to spectacular. Shop till you drop, and live your passion for handbags, to get a lock on being in style year-round.

Accessories

⬜ **Bagborroworsteal.com.** If you are starting to save for your big day and don't want to spend a lot of money, but you still want to look great when you go out, you can avail yourself of a number of consignment-type stores that are popping up all over the place. Bagborroworsteal.com is a good place to check out accessories from handbags to jewelry to sunglasses. You can "borrow" chic designer items for a small fraction of the cost and give them back when you are done. It's like gaining a closet full of red-carpet accessories without breaking the bank.

• • • • • • • • • • • • •   **FUN STUFF**   • • • • • • • • • • • • • •

Lingerie

⬜ **Hankypanky.com.** The mission statement of this site is: indulge your inner flirt. That's exactly what we think all girls should do, whether you are 25 years old or 75 years old. With offerings from lingerie to thongs to bridal items, this is a perfect place to play. Breathe easy: with these adornments, *sexy* doesn't mean *uncomfortable*. Hanky Panky prides itself on making you "feel how comfortable sexy can be!"

Essentials

Bootyparlor.com. Fun, fabulous, and never intimidating: that is the motto at Booty Parlor, which has become many girls' favorite place to shop for sexy essentials and bedroom accessories. Whether it's for a special "date night," a relaxing evening at home, or a crazy romp on the town, this is the place you need to visit. Booty Parlor is making women feel sexy no matter where they are!

ADVICE

WhyHasntHe.com. When it comes to love, relationships, dating, and understanding men, you are never alone. WhyHasntHe.com is your source for all of your relationship needs. Whether you are walking to a date or walking down the aisle, we are here for you every step of the way. WhyHasntHe.com is brought to you by Matt Titus and Tamsen Fadal, a real couple giving real relationship advice.

REFERENCES

•••••••••••••••◄ CHAPTER 1 ►•••••••••••••••

The Associated Press. "Divorce Rate Falls to Lowest Level Since 1970." Msnbc.com (May 10, 2007).

Jayson, Sharon. "More View Cohabitation as Acceptable Choice." *USA Today* (June 9, 2008).

Kimball, Michele Bush. "Relationships: Waiting to Marry May Improve Your Chance at Marital Success." Divorce360.com (2008).

Popenoe, David. "Cohabitation, Marriage and Child Well-Being." *The National Marriage Project*, Rutgers University (2008).

Roberts, Sam. "51% of Women are Now Living Without Spouse." *New York Times* (January 16, 2007).

Steinhauer, Jennifer. "Studies Find Big Benefits in Marriage." *New York Times* (April 10, 1995).

• • • • • • • • • • • • • ◦ CHAPTER 2 ◦ • • • • • • • • • • • • •

Popenoe, David. "Cohabitation, Marriage and Child Well-Being." *The National Marriage Project*, Rutgers University (2008).

• • • • • • • • • • • • • ◦ CHAPTER 3 ◦ • • • • • • • • • • • • •

Knowledge@wharton. "To Love, Honor, Cherish and Consume: The Selling of the American Wedding." Knowledge@wharton (June 25, 2008).

• • • • • • • • • • • • • ◦ CHAPTER 5 ◦ • • • • • • • • • • • • •

Marchant, Joanna. "Sex, Lies and Monogamy." *New Scientist* (April 28, 2001).
Thenest.com. "Sexy Movies to Set the Mood." Thenest.com (July 7, 2008).

• • • • • • • • • • • • • ◦ CHAPTER 6 ◦ • • • • • • • • • • • • •

Straus, Jillian. "Lone Stars: Being Single." *Psychology Today* (May/June 2006).

CHAPTER 7

George, Alison. "Love Special: Secrets of Long-Term Love." *New Scientist* (April 29, 2006).

INDEX

ABOUT THE AUTHORS

Matt Titus and Tamsen Fadal are the founders of Matt's Little Black Book, a Manhattan matchmaking agency and relationship coaching service that caters to the nation's single, successful, and selective men and women. The husband-and-wife duo are known for their honest, straight-from-the-hip advice that helps singles find true love and helps couples overcome the everyday challenges they face.

Their first book, *Why Hasn't He Called?*, garnered national attention from millions of women as well as the major media.

Matt is a regular contributor on "Tyra" and CBS's "The Early Show." He has also appeared on "Martha Stewart," "The Morning Show with Mike and Juliet," E!, and The Style Network, among other outlets. He is contributor to *OK!* magazine and also writes for the Huffington Post.

Matt and Tamsen were featured in their own reality series, Lifetime's "Matched in Manhattan," a behind-the-scenes look at their lives and their business as successful "dating agents" and relationship experts. They are also the founders of WhyHasntHe.com, a website that helps women understand men, dating, and relationships. They answer questions daily, offering honest insight from a real couple helping real women navigate the fun but sometimes confusing world of dating and relationships.

A TV journalist, Tamsen not only adds a female perspective to Matt's advice but also works with him to share the secrets that helped them become a couple.

Tamsen started as a journalist, most recently working as a lifestyle reporter with her own segment, "Totally Tamsen," at WPIX-TV in New York City. She received an Emmy Award in 2005 for Outstanding Investigative Journalist and was also nominated for two Emmy Awards in 2004 for her investigative work. She has traveled to London to cover the U.K. bombings and to Afghanistan to cover the war on terror.

On a personal level, Tamsen and Matt are active in causes to raise awareness of breast cancer and ovarian cancer, having lost both their mothers to the disease.

They reside in Manhattan with their two Chihuahuas, Matsen and Parker.